WHAT YOUR COLLEAGUES ARE SAYING .

D1220254

"This is an amazing book. While it is designed to build everyone's capacity to teach in distance learning environments, it is truly a primer on effective teaching in postsecondary education. Educators who utilize these clear and practical suggestions will see their students achieve stronger learning outcomes. *The Distance Learning Playbook for College and University Instruction* should be a cornerstone of faculty professional development efforts."

—**Joseph F. Johnson, Jr., PhD,** Executive Director of the National Center for Urban School Transformation and Emeritus Dean and Professor of San Diego State University

"*The Distance Learning Playbook for College and University Instruction* is a very useful guide to helping educators make the transition from onsite to online teaching. The highly respected authors skillfully demonstrate how teachers can apply evidence-based practices from more traditional learning environments to a rapidly evolving world of online learning. The result is a wonderful self-guided tour of extraordinary opportunities to close the distance for learners."

—**David W. Andrews, PhD,** President of National University

"*The Distance Learning Playbook for College and University Instruction* offers an innovative learner-centered approach to student achievement where self-care, social emotional learning, instructional clarity, and responsive leadership strategies converge to support faculty in facilitating learner experiences that continue to transition students from 'passenger to active driver' in all learning environments, including distance education."

—**Robert N. Corley III, PhD,** Associate Vice-Provost for Academic Affairs of Virginia State University and Project Director of the Wallace Foundation UPPI

"*The Distance Learning Playbook for College and University Instruction* by Douglas Fisher, Nancy Frey, John Almarode, and John Hattie is a timely and necessary addition to every faculty's library. The authors' considerate and experiential approach to distance learning provides a well-researched foundation, authentic vignettes of instructors' experiences, easily accessible video and web links, and helpful techniques that can be used among most disciplines. Impressively, they envisage the distance learning environment beginning with the instructor and as an active, dynamic, and engaging space for learning and teaching."

—**Arlette Willis,** Professor of Curriculum and Instruction at University of Illinois at Urbana-Champaign

"These authors once again exceed expectations with this thought-provoking and very practical guide to distance learning. The timing could not be better. Higher education faculty and administrators will find it extremely useful—including a much-needed chapter on self-care, a topic often overlooked in the literature. The pointers on engaging and assessing students are particularly helpful, and the learning intentions and success criteria make this an indispensable resource for new and veteran online instructors alike."

—**James P. Frazee, EdD,** Chief Academic Technology Officer and Associate Vice President for Learning Technologies & Environments, San Diego State University

THE

DISTANCE
LEARNING
PLAYBOOK FOR
COLLEGE & UNIVERSITY
INSTRUCTION

THE DISTANCE LEARNING PLAYBOOK FOR COLLEGE & UNIVERSITY INSTRUCTION

TEACHING FOR ENGAGEMENT & IMPACT IN ANY SETTING

DOUGLAS FISHER
NANCY FREY
JOHN ALMARODE
JOHN HATTIE

CORWIN | SAGE

FOR INFORMATION:

Corwin
A SAGE Company
2455 Teller Road
Thousand Oaks, California 91320
(800) 233-9936
www.corwin.com

SAGE Publications Ltd.
1 Oliver's Yard
55 City Road
London EC1Y 1SP
United Kingdom

SAGE Publications India Pvt. Ltd.
B 1/I 1 Mohan Cooperative Industrial Area
Mathura Road, New Delhi 110 044
India

SAGE Publications Asia-Pacific Pte. Ltd.
18 Cross Street #10-10/11/12
China Square Central
Singapore 048423

Editorial Director: Monica Eckman
Director and Publisher,
Corwin Classroom: Lisa Luedeke
Editorial Development Manager: Julie Nemer
Associate Content
Development Editor: Sharon Wu
Production Editor: Melanie Birdsall
Copy Editor: Diane DiMura
Typesetter: C&M Digitals (P) Ltd.
Proofreader: Theresa Kay
Indexer: Molly Hall
Cover Designer: Gail Buschman
Interior Designer: Rose Storey
Marketing Manager: Deena Meyer

Module-opening images courtesy of iStock.com/Eoneren

Printed in the United States of America

ISBN 978-1-0718-3867-9

Library of Congress Control Number: 2020915951

This book is printed on acid-free paper.

20 21 22 23 24 10 9 8 7 6 5 4 3 2 1

CONTENTS

Note: The term *teacher* is utilized in the headings of two chapters that are rooted in Visible Learning® research. *Teacher* is representative of teaching in all contexts. With respect to teacher credibility specifically, the original research was conducted at the college level.

Visit the companion website at
resources.corwin.com/DLPlaybook-college
for downloadable resources and videos.

LIST OF VIDEOS

Note From the Publisher: The authors have provided video and web content throughout the book that is available to you through QR (quick response) codes. To read a QR code, you must have a smartphone or tablet with a camera. We recommend that you download a QR code reader app that is made specifically for your phone or tablet brand.

Videos may also be accessed at **resources.corwin.com/DLPlaybook-college**

ACKNOWLEDGMENTS

The distance learning playbooks were the brainchild of Elena Nikitina at Corwin, who proposed the original idea that energized everyone as a way to collaboratively support teaching and learning, distance or otherwise. This book would not exist without the tireless efforts of our amazing editor, Lisa Luedeke, who mobilized the collective effort needed to bring it to life. We are grateful to both of you for your vision and can-do attitude.

We are also grateful to our colleagues from colleges and universities around the country who were willing to share their approaches to distance learning. Thank you!

INTRODUCTION

Higher education changed across college and university campuses in the middle of the spring semester in 2020. For those faculty members not already engaged in online learning, this change was abrupt and jarring. Although there are a growing number of fully online or distance learning degree granting institutions, in the fall of 2018 students enrolled in exclusively distance education courses accounted for only 16.6 percent of the total enrollment at postsecondary institutions (NCES, 2019). This includes undergraduate, graduate, public, and private. Only 18.7 percent of the student population in higher education were enrolled in at least one distance education course (NCES, 2019). There is now an expectation that the other 64.7 percent of students not enrolled in any distance learning course will learn from a distance. Whether they are majoring in anthropology or architecture, biblical studies or business, nanoscience or nursing, this expectation may involve learning be fully at a distance or a blend of online and within the storied halls of an academic building. Who knows what higher education will be like in the short term? In any case, we hope that those of us that have always engaged in teaching and learning on campus will return better than before, taking ideas that we implemented during pandemic teaching and applying them in new situations. The constant across all college and university campuses, one that we share with those postsecondary institutions that have always been fully online, remains the same: to ensure that students are learning. We suspect that the future will include increased amounts of distance learning. Faculty have embraced their responsibility to impact learning, irrespective of the format of their course and programs of study. Let's seize on what we have learned to improve postsecondary education in any format, whether face to face or from a distance.

College and university faculty across the globe have stepped up and continued to teach and mentor their students as they pursue their program of study that will prepare them to graduate and enter the workforce or postbaccalaureate education. Whether we teach a 4/4 load or a 2/1, we are still responsible for fostering, nurturing, and sustaining the interest and engagement of our students through distance learning as they prepare for the next step in their professional careers. From our home workspaces, we continued to motivate our students (mostly) to engage in thoughtful inquiry and discourse that continue to make the struggle of learning joyful. We have continued to provide feedback on problem-solving sets, papers, and capstone projects at the right time and in the right way to each student so as not to "do" the work for the students. Faculty know where to go next and how to balance the breadth and depth of the content. We have re-purposed our know-how to invest in the "after class work" of grading, preparing for the next class meeting, developing resources, and still maintaining our scholarship and service requirements.

The world changed in early 2020. And we'd like to take a moment to acknowledge the heroic efforts of PreK–16 educators worldwide who, during a

Doug Fisher (San Diego State University, Educational Leadership) introduces the goals of this version of the book.

resources.corwin.com/ DLPlaybook-college

To read a QR code, you must have a smartphone or tablet with a camera. We recommend that you download a QR code reader app that is made specifically for your phone or tablet brand.

pandemic, used what they knew to create meaningful learning experiences for students. In most cases, we didn't miss a beat. Like the health-care workers who rose to the challenge, faculty stepped up and made sure that students continued to learn. We didn't say that it was easy. And we didn't say that we wanted to learn this way. But learn we did. And now that we did learn, it's time to plan for distance learning using what we know now. Again, the 64.7 percent of students not enrolled in any distance learning course in 2019 will likely learn from a distance in the 2020–2021 academic year.

To be clear, the pandemic teaching of 2020 was really not distance learning. It was also not an independent study from March to May. Independent study students still have the option to sit down one-on-one and engage in face-to-face teaching and mentoring. That is not what happened here. We found ourselves leaving for Spring Break one day and abruptly transitioning to crisis teaching one week later. With that behind us, we now have time to be more purposeful and intentional with distance learning. What should not be lost is that as a field we learned more about what works by at times experiencing what didn't work in a remote learning environment. It heightened our sense of what we already knew in face-to-face classrooms (Hattie, 2018):

- Fostering student self-regulation is crucial for moving learning to deep and transfer levels.

- Learning accelerates when the student, not the faculty member, is taught to be in control of learning.

- There needs to be a diversity of instructional approaches (not just some video lectures or narrated slide decks and then some off-line independent work).

- Well-designed peer learning impacts understanding.

- Feedback in a high-trust environment must be integrated into the learning cycle.

TO BE CLEAR, THE PANDEMIC TEACHING OF 2020 WAS REALLY NOT DISTANCE LEARNING. IT WAS CRISIS TEACHING.

Let's use what we have learned and are continuing to learn whether in a face-to-face or distance learning environment. As a part of face-to-face teaching, let's build our students' capacity (and our own) for distance learning. Now we have time to use evidence about what works best to impact students. And that's the purpose of this book—to apply the wisdom of **Visible Learning**® research to distance learning. But before we do so, we need to acknowledge the potential differential impact of distance learning on students.

A VISIBLE LEARNING® PRIMER

There exists a significant amount of published research about teaching and learning, and more studies are produced each year. Many of these studies come from our very institutions, conducted by our colleagues across campus, down the hall, or in our own research group. Who doesn't want to make research- or evidence-based decisions about teaching and learning? It's hard to sift through to figure out what to do. It seems that everything "works" so any choice we make seems reasonable. Every colleague has their preferred way of teaching and staunchly defends that preferred way in department meetings. But the fact of the matter is that some things work *best* in accelerating students' learning. Thus, it's useful to know what works best to accelerate students' learning and leverage that knowledge in our distance learning environment.

Enter the Visible Learning database. It's easily accessible at www.visiblelearningmetax.com. This database focuses on meta-analyses, or aggregations of studies, to determine the impact that specific actions or influences have on students' learning. These meta-analyses use an effect size, which is a statistical tool to scale the impact. To date, the database includes over 1,800 meta-analyses with over 300 million students. The average impact on students' learning from all the things we do is 0.40 (effect size). Thus, influences over 0.40 are above average and should accelerate students' learning. Those below are less likely to ensure that students learn a full year of stuff for a year of school. That does not mean we ignore those influences below 0.40, but rather we are cautious and we think about ways that we implement those practices.

John Almarode (James Madison University, Education) explains the principles of Visible Learning.

resources.corwin.com/ DLPlaybook-college

You may have heard about the Visible Learning database and, through a quick search on the internet, see that many of the results of that search reference the PreK–12 classroom. Although much attention has been given to the translation and implementation of the specific actions or influences into PreK–12 classrooms, there are a considerable number of meta-analyses that come from studies of teaching and learning in higher education. For example, the effect size for problem-based learning draws from several meta-analyses in the college classroom, health sciences, pharmacy, nursing, and medicine (e.g., Sayyah, Shirbandi, & Rahim, 2017).

Let's consider a few additional examples. Are you surprised that students' prior achievement is related to their future achievement? The effect size is 0.59. Yes, students who have achieved in the past are likely to achieve in the future. The database confirms what we expect. Are you surprised that boredom has a negative effect on learning? The effect size is –0.47. Learning opportunities are lost when students are bored. There is a logic to the evidence summarized in the Visible Learning database, right?

As another example, the instructional strategy jigsaw has an effect size of 1.20. Powerful! It should work to accelerate student learning. Our personal experiences with this approach, when implemented correctly, confirm it. But, since we are talking about distance learning, it's important to note that none of the jigsaw studies collected for any of the meta-analyses were done from afar. In this case, we'll have to leverage our teaching expertise and identify the essential components of a jigsaw and determine how it can be used online.

Several themes are at the heart of Visible Learning.

1. **The first is that a faculty member's investment in learning means that there is a drive to foster each student's increasing ability to recognize when they are learning, when they are not, and how to go about**

fixing it. With distance learning, we must foster this type of agency in our undergraduates. That means that teacher clarity (clarity about the learning) and feedback are crucial. You will find separate modules devoted to these two things elsewhere in this book.

2. **The second theme is that faculty members seek to know the impact of their instruction in terms of progress and achievement and take steps to refine their approaches.** That means that we have methods for discovering what students already know in order to minimize wasted instructional time such that we can focus on needed learning experiences. Further, the individual student is the unit of analysis—we know what works, what works when, and what works for whom.

3. **The third theme is that the mindframes of faculty members, which is to say dispositions and beliefs, are in the driver's seat.** That means that we collaborate with one another, talk about learning more than teaching, and invest in relationships with our students and colleagues in order to be an agent of change.

These themes transcend the delivery method. Whether face-to-face with students or in virtual or distance environments, these themes endure. On the facing page, take a few minutes to reflect on these themes and note how you accomplish these in face-to-face classes. Then consider what these might look like in virtual spaces.

VISIBLE LEARNING AND DISTANCE LEARNING

This brings us to the effect size of distance learning itself. We know the effect size of technology remains low and has been so for the last fifty years. As Dylan Wiliam has often said, technology is the revolution that is still coming! The effect of distance learning is small (0.14) but that does not mean it is NOT effective—it means it does not matter whether teachers undertake teaching in situ or from a distance over the internet (or, like when John started in his first university, via the post office). What we *do* matters, not the medium of doing it.

There are some technology elements that are worth attending to. The highest effects of digital technology are interactive videos (0.54), intelligent tutoring systems (0.51), in writing (0.42), and in mathematics (0.35). The lowest effects are the presence of mobile phones (at −0.34, please turn them off), and the presence of one-on-one laptops (0.16). Of course, the studies that were used to calculate the effect sizes involved purposeful and planned learning in virtual or distance environments and in face-to-face classrooms, not crisis pandemic teaching.

NOTE TO SELF

How do you enact these themes in face-to-face classrooms? How can they occur in virtual classrooms?

THEME	FACE-TO-FACE SETTINGS	VIRTUAL/DISTANCE SETTINGS
Teacher clarity and feedback is used to fuel students' ability to become their own teachers—take ownership of their learning.		
Methods for measuring the impact of teaching are used to understand each student's progress *and* achievement, with adjustments to teaching made accordingly.		
Investment in collaboration with adults and relationships with students is continuous.		

 Download forms throughout the book at **resources.corwin.com/DLPlaybook-college**.

John Hattie (University of Melbourne, Education) talks about distance learning in higher education and what's different.

resources.corwin.com/ DLPlaybook-college

IT IS THE CHOICE OF TASKS RELATIVE TO WHERE OUR LEARNERS ARE NOW AND WHERE THEY NEED TO GO NEXT THAT ADVANCES THEIR LEARNING.

When people see that there is an effect size of 0.14, they incorrectly assume that distance learning is not effective. But let's take a closer look. In comparison with traditional building-based learning, distance learning is not an accelerator. It's also not negative. That means that the setting isn't the deciding factor. Nor should it be interpreted that "distance is disastrous." What is far more important are the methods of instruction that spark learning, not the medium. Consider what some of those technologies with higher effect sizes have to offer. Interactive videos require students to engage in active learning, not just passive viewing (something students do in classrooms, too). Intelligent tutoring systems provide rapid feedback and customized instruction based on what the learner knows and doesn't know. Similarly, high-performing classroom teachers use responsive feedback and instruction that reduces teaching what is already known in favor of what needs to be known next.

The choice of task matters critically. It is the choice of tasks relative to where students are now and where they need to go next that advances their learning.

- Use technology for great diagnosis of what students need to learn.

- Share scoring rubrics and success criteria up front with students before they get too involved in the task.

- Be clear. Clarity about learning matters more when students are not in front of you to correct, cajole, and to give instant feedback. You cannot immediately evaluate progress as you do in the physical classroom.

- Build formative evaluation opportunities into the tasks.

We need to view technology use like planning for next week's class and creating resources: It is the means and starting point, not the core, of teaching. It is the decisions we make as students are learning, as we listen to them think aloud, as we give them alternate strategies and help them work with others to jointly advance learning, as we formatively evaluate our impact, that are important.

- Optimize the social interaction aspects (we do not want to be talked at, but learn with).

- Check for understanding (listen to the feedback from the students about their learning even more when you do not have the usual cues of the classrooms).

- Make sure there is a balance between the precious knowledge and the deep thinking (too often online favors the former over the latter).

Bottom line: Understand what it means to be a learner online. When the usual peer interactions are often not as present, the faculty member's observational skills are different, and there is too often an overemphasis on content and repetition.

REFLECTIVE WRITING

This is just for you. What new connections are you making between teaching and learning in face-to-face environments and in distance learning environments? What do your students need to know and be able to do to function well in both mediums?

A QUESTION OF EQUITY

Students whose learning has been traditionally compromised in our colleges and universities remain at risk in distance learning. This includes English learners; students with disabilities; students who live in poverty; those from traditionally underrepresented ethnic and racial groups; students who identify as gay, lesbian, bisexual, or transgender; and those who have experienced significant trauma. Colleges, universities, and faculty members should redouble their efforts to ensure that the needs of these students are met. Our universities (San Diego State University, James Madison University, and The University of Melbourne) devoted significant time and energy to meet the equity needs of our students at a distance.

TECHNOLOGY USE IS THE MEANS AND STARTING POINT, NOT THE CORE, OF TEACHING.

- Meet students' basic needs.
- Ensure equitable access to learning resources.
- Proactively design responsive, restorative structures.

But there are students who may not have been considered in the past who are also at risk when it comes to distance learning, including students

- Who struggle with low self-regulation and are highly dependent on the structure provide by face-to-face classes and the various services offered on campus for academic support or student services

- Who return with high levels of stress and social and emotional concerns

- With limited proficiency in using quality learning strategies and guidance necessary to promote development

- Who already had a lack of progress in their program of study for whatever reason

- Who have low concepts of themselves as learners

- Who lack proficiency in the critical reading and numeracy skills needed to move to the next level—particularly first-year students or freshmen as they engage in their first postsecondary courses or general education courses and are thus more likely to become part of the "Matthew effect" in which the rich get richer while the poor get poorer (Stanovich, 1986)

- Living at home where they are confronted with challenges related to their parents or guardians, siblings, and others; there will be an exacerbation of physical and emotional health issues

- With parents or guardians who now unexpectedly have limited financial capacity to provide the necessary financial support while at home.

All students, and especially those who are at greater risk of not making expected progress, must be targeted for proactive supports that address their equity needs and build their capacity to learn at a distance. Throughout this book, we include examples of ways that faculty can address the needs of these students and work to ensure that the equity gains that have been realized are not lost. In addition, we see distance learning as an opportunity to engage students in different ways and potentially address some of the needs that they have that could not have been met in traditional classes. We want to promote the notion that what we have learned through the research evidence of distance learning (not just our recent emergency efforts) should be leveraged to improve teaching in virtual environments. We also want to advocate that what we have learned through the research evidence on learning in any environment should inform our future efforts and improve our readiness, as well as our students' capacity, to continue their postsecondary education regardless of the setting.

We are still active faculty members, committed to teaching, scholarship, and service. The unexpected transition to remote learning doesn't mean we no longer know how to teach. We can still impact the lives of our students and know that we made a difference. We hope that this playbook provides you with examples of familiar tasks and ideas that you can mobilize at a distance to ensure students learn.

Nancy Frey (San Diego State University, Educational Leadership) delivers a message to our colleagues.

resources.corwin.com/ DLPlaybook-college

MODULE 1
SELF-CARE

LEARNING INTENTIONS

- I am learning that my own self-care is necessary for the transition to virtual and distance learning.

- I am learning about the impact of trauma on educators.

SUCCESS CRITERIA

- I can identify a place to work.

- I can practice my routines and manage my schedule.

- I have at least one connected conversation per day with someone outside of my home.

- I have a plan for my personal well-being.

- I recognize the signs of trauma and compassion fatigue.

Perhaps you're surprised that we start a book about distance learning with the recommendation that you need to take care of yourself. But hear us out. If you burn out, if you become exhausted and overwhelmed, you're no good to your students (much less your family, friends, let alone yourself). The vast majority of us did not sign up for this type of teaching. We had images of ourselves arriving for our Monday morning 8:00 a.m. class to be greeted by the faces of eager learners who could not wait to see us. Yeah, we laughed at that sentence as well. Let's try this again. We had images of working with advisees, students in our majors section, first-year students exploring possible majors and minors, greeted by faces that were ready to engage in learning. There would be rich discussions around British literature, experiments in the alternative fuels building, and collective learning in the nursing simulation laboratory. We would continue to meet with our research group, have conversations with our colleagues about the next grant, manuscript, or conference presentation. Of course, we often choose to take work home with us, perhaps to write, plan, or grade, but there was a separation between work and home. Distance learning can interrupt all of those routines. So, before we engage in distance learning, we need to take care of ourselves. As our friend and colleague Ricky Robertson reminds us, follow the instructions of the flight attendant and put your oxygen mask on first before helping others.

You'll find that in each module in this playbook, we invite you first to draw on your own expertise. Although you may be new to distance learning, you aren't new to education. You have been a student and now you are a faculty member. And prior knowledge, which is an aspect of prior achievement, has a strong influence on new learning if it is properly leveraged. In fact, learning strategies that integrate prior knowledge with new learning have a strong influence, with an effect size of 0.93 (Hattie, 2018). Consider this an invitation to activate your prior knowledge to develop new ideas.

DRAWING ON MY EXPERTISE

How do you maintain a work–life balance? How can you do so when working from home? How do you do so when working on campus?

For the vast majority of us, our first experience at distance learning started as a result of the global pandemic COVID-19. This book is not just about that. It's about developing and delivering quality distance learning experiences for students—anywhere, anytime. But we would be remiss if we did not acknowledge the initiation of this type of teaching. Who could have imagined that we would be sheltering in place, anxious about a monster that could harm us or our loved ones? But the current crisis is just the most recent, albeit major, trauma we have experienced. Unlike other traumatic experiences, this one is global and has touched every member of the human race. There is some comfort in that, but it's still difficult and surreal. It also makes us stop to think about the other traumas we have experienced. You see, trauma is not just something that happens to "them"— our students or other people. It's hard to imagine a person who has reached the age of 25 who hasn't experienced at least one adverse childhood event:

- Divorce
- Death of a loved one
- A loved one incarcerated
- Community violence
- Poverty
- Exposure to domestic violence
- Living with someone who has mental illness or who is suicidal
- Alcohol or drug addiction in the home

ALTHOUGH YOU MAY BE NEW TO DISTANCE LEARNING, YOU AREN'T NEW TO EDUCATION.

We carry that trauma with us, as Van der Kolk noted in the title of his 2015 book, *The Body Keeps the Score*. By that, he meant that traumatic experiences inevitably leave their traces on our minds, emotions, and even on our physical health. We all have those traces and some of us have yet to address the impact. That's why social and emotional learning needs to continue with adults and does not end upon graduation from high school. And, as we noted earlier, additional traumatic experiences accumulate throughout our lives.

It's important to acknowledge the issue. An ostrich approach is not useful. Instead, colleges and universities can engage in social and emotional learning for adults, if for no other reason than the fact that faculty members model behaviors that students mimic. When we model healthy, growth-producing relationships, students see how they work. When we model respect, kindness, and a range of emotions, students notice how we regulate and respond. But even more important, we believe, is the opportunity to help adults continue their social and emotional learning journey and become happier, healthier members of the community, both at college or university and in the wider community.

TRAUMA IS PART OF OUR LIVES, AND WE DON'T WANT TO EXACERBATE IT DURING DISTANCE LEARNING EFFORTS.

Yes, that got deep, but we want to recognize that trauma is part of our lives and don't want to exacerbate it during distance learning efforts. There are a number of recommendations, based on evidence from other stressful times in the lives of humans as well as long-term "work at home" studies, that we can use to inform and take care of ourselves. We will chunk these into some groups and provide you an opportunity to consider your plan. The first is about your workspace at home. The recommendations are to

- Keep a dedicated workspace.
- Set ground rules with the people in your space.

The dedicated office space does not have to be a home office. That's not what we mean. But rather, a place where you can easily teach and engage students. Sarah Westcraver, a mathematics professor, set up a space in the spare bedroom of her apartment. This allowed her to adjust the surrounding environment (e.g., the background, lighting) for her classes, virtual office hours, university committee meetings, and department meetings.

"The spare bedroom is ideal because there are several windows for great lighting. Plus, when I am ready to stop for the day, I can simply leave the spare bedroom, close the door, and truly step away from work." Dr. Westcraver points out that the spare bedroom, which is not used that often, gives her the latitude to redesign her surroundings. "I can move things out of the visual field of the computer camera. I have also propped up a dry erase board that has information related to the classes I am teaching this semester. For mathematics, having this dry erase board is important."

Louis Shiekel, an exercise science professor, is fortunate enough to have a home office space. In fact, he brought his standing desk home from his office in the exercise science department. "When I'm talking with students, I'm used to standing. This just feels more natural to me," he says. "I think I project better when I stand and I'm amazed at how much they watch me. I don't talk the whole time, but when I do, I prefer to stand." In addition, Mr. Shiekel has his desk facing the door to the home office. This allows him to see if his young children walk into the room before they enter the visual field of his computer camera. "I also like to be able to close the door. When I am in private conversations with students and colleagues, I want to protect their confidentiality when necessary. There are times I simply need to close the door and ensure that my family allows that time to work directly with students and colleagues."

In addition to having a dedicated space in your living environment to teach, it's important to set ground rules with the others who live in the home or apartment. Of course, we all understand the child who needs something and interrupts a live class meeting or the pet that jumps up on the table and walks in front of the computer. It's just that your stress level can be reduced when you have clear guidelines for people. Dr. Westcraver asks that people in her home text her to let her know that they're coming into the spare bedroom so she is not surprised. Mr. Shiekel asks his family not to play around his workspace so that things are not moved. The family has agreed to restrict laundry days to the weekend or in the evening so that the machines are not running while he is working.

NOTE TO SELF

My dedicated workspace is

_____

_____

_____

_____

I need to have the following items near me:

_____

_____

_____

_____

My virtual background is a blank wall, a picture of my regular class, something not too distracting for my students.

Guidelines that I need to share with others when working from home include

- _____

- _____

- _____

- _____

The second group of recommendations focuses on routines and includes that you

- Create a morning routine.

- Maintain regular hours.

- Schedule breaks.

- End your day with a routine.

Routines are useful for us as they help us organize, plan, and predict. One of the risks with distance learning is that our routines are disrupted, and we are not sure how to reestablish them. In future modules, we'll focus on routines for students. For now, we need to focus on the routines for us as faculty.

The longer we have been in our position at the college or university, the greater the likelihood that we have routines. For example, do you have a specific routine you go through before class? What about on your writing days? These routines were important to us before the pandemic and they are important to us now. We just have to adapt them for our current context. Michel Leonard, a business professor, has incorporated routines into his home working environment. "On campus, I have to park quite a bit away from my office. That walk from my car to the office is where I used to think through my plan for the day. Now, working from home, I simulate that walk time each morning by taking a walk through my neighborhood first thing in the morning." This fifteen-minute walk helps him clear his head and prepare for his classes and his focus for the day. "During the day, I set aside time for lunch, breaks during the day. Although I can't walk down the hall and engage in a discussion with my colleagues, I can set aside time during the day to have a cup of tea or call a colleague and have a virtual discussion." At the end of the day, Dr. Leonard points out that he has to simulate the walk back to his car. As you might have guessed, he takes a fifteen-minute walk at the end of the day. "In addition to the physical walk, mentally the walk closes out the day. Unless it is absolutely necessary, I do not go back into my home office after the walk. The walk symbolizes the end of the day."

Claudia Readwright is an instructional coach in the Fresno Unified School District in California, specializing in primary education. You may be asking why someone specializing in primary education is included in this book. There is a lesson to be learned from all of our colleagues, including those in primary education.

A VIEW FROM THE EARLY YEARS

We have been invited to activate our prior knowledge in order to develop new ideas. I thought it prudent to take a lesson from the Mister Roger's playbook. If we employ a visual cue that signals the beginning and ending of our workday, it can serve as a reminder to our students and ourselves. Mister Rogers enters his "television house," removes and hangs up his jacket, then changes out of his street shoes into his sneakers. Our own routines should similarly aid us in bracketing our workdays. Apply your early learning lens to yourself, as you know how important it is to continue our own social and emotional learning journey.

Routines make students feel welcome and included, and the same applies to us as adults. Striking yoga poses or other gentle movement activities, accompanied by peaceful music, is a way to engage with yourself first thing in the morning. Other early morning routines might include a short walk, a few quiet minutes outside on your porch or balcony, or listening to a favorite podcast while you get ready.

Some of the "Work at Home" recommendations are easy enough to implement and echo what we teach our own students. How might you set up a dedicated workspace? Maybe that could include a trifold science board created to look like the mini focus board you have in your physical classroom. It could include the focus of the day's class (e.g., protein synthesis, goal-means gap theory, the cultural context surround the works of Andy Warhol), a particular type of mathematics problem, a visual model of a diesel engine, or a news clipping that will drive the class discussion. It is a manageable size, portable, and can be folded flat if needed. Having your daily teaching items easily available to you can lower your stress level when teaching online.

How might we establish ground rules in our shared space? Your family and your pets are an important part of your life, just as they are for the children we teach. Set up a signal with your family that shows when you'll be teaching in a live session—perhaps a kind note on the door. A hat or crown reminds others this is a time for no interruptions (barring emergencies, of course). And if a family member or pet wanders into the camera frame, anyway, introduce them. You're modeling for your own students how we handle unexpected interruptions in ways that are graceful and kind.

Four focus areas have given our early learning team time to reflect and steer our self-care efforts in a positive direction. For a Health benefit, try including at least forty minutes of daily exercise, three days a week. In the Love category, include doing something just for you. By stepping out of your comfort zone, and trying something new, you can gain a sense of Competence. If we focus on demonstrating our thankfulness, we may notice our Gratitude quotient grows. In addition, weekly check-ins with colleagues are often productive in sharing common challenges and generating new ideas.

Close your workday with an emotional check-in. Celebrate what you have accomplished and set a small goal for tomorrow. Remember that making each class meeting successful for students starts with you being you. Then hang up your cardigan for the day and know that you've done well.

By Claudia Readwright

Dr. Leonard may take a fifteen-minute walk at the end of the day while Mister Rogers hangs up his cardigan. Both gentlemen have a routine that helps keep a work–life balance when the distance between work and life is mere steps and not a commute.

Now, highlight one morning routine option and one end-of-day routine and try them for two weeks. If it's not helping you, change it up and try something else. But for the sake of your family, your students, and your well-being, find some routines that work and use them regularly.

NOTE TO SELF

MY MORNING ROUTINE OPTIONS	WHEN I WILL TAKE BREAKS	MY END-OF-DAY ROUTINE OPTIONS

The third group of recommendations focuses on socialization opportunities. We are professionals, and professionals socialize with other professionals. There are a number of options for doing this, including online and off-line activities. When we are teaching at a distance, we need to remember that we need to socialize with people outside of our homes and keep actively engaged in our friend networks. We thrive on both personal and professional connections and we should not forget this necessity as we teach from a distance. Thus, you should consider opportunities to

- Socialize with colleagues.
- Have a connected and meaningful conversation each day with someone outside of your home.

Marsha Alvarez, a social psychologist, strives to engage with colleagues and individuals outside of her home on a regular basis. "Not only do I set up times to talk to my research team, my department has faculty social hours that allow us to simply engage with each other. Plus, the university offers multiple professional learning opportunities. I try to attend those on a regular basis. For example,

Mathew Mansoor (Cuyamaca Community College, Psychology) talks about striking a work–life balance.

resources.corwin.com/ DLPlaybook-college

I have signed up for professional learning workshops on different tools to use that keep students engaged in the learning." As we move forward with remote learning, take some time and identify opportunities offered by the college or university that promote socialization with colleagues and provide connected and meaningful conversations with individuals outside of your home.

Melissa Reichert has created an online community that includes her collaborators from across the country. "We set up virtual coffee breaks that are focused on something we read or came across in our work. This could be a recent published article or a book we are reading. In either case, we set aside 30 minutes each day as if we all worked in the same building and were gathering around the coffee pot." These can be video calls or voice calls. "These conversations prevent me from feeling isolated and at the same time prevent the distance learning from putting a damper on our identity as scholars."

Your turn. Take a look at the prompt below—how will you socialize with colleagues and ensure that you have one meaningful, connected conversation each day with someone outside of your home?

NOTE TO SELF

My social connection plan includes

_____

_____

_____

_____

_____

_____

_____

_____

_____

_____

_____

_____

_____

In addition to the three groups of personal support discussed above, it's important for people to take care of themselves physically. Managing our stress, eating healthily, and exercising regularly are important to our well-being.

Your turn. What can you do to support your well-being?

NOTE TO SELF

My plan for stress management

_____

_____

_____

_____

My plan for healthy eating

_____

_____

_____

_____

My plan for getting regular sleep

_____

_____

_____

_____

My exercise plan

_____

_____

_____

_____

See, it wasn't that hard. But we know that developing a wellness plan is only part of it. Having a commitment partner increases the likelihood that you will actually implement your plans. Robert McCauley, a philosophy and religion professor, shared that setting up a plan is easy, but implementing the plan is not. "If I did not have a collaborator that could hold me accountable, I am not sure what I would do. There are so many days that I plan on reaching out to colleagues, but I decide it would be better to grade one more essay, edit my slide deck one more time, or take care of one last writing task before the end of the day. Then, the next thing I know it is 7:00 p.m. and I am still sitting at my desk in the living room." When Robert learned about the value of commitment partners, he contacted one of his coauthors on several articles and asked if they could check in with each other each week. "I knew that I would have to answer to Rachele, so I would really do it. But it turns out, I really like what I decided to do and was super happy to talk with her and share our progress on our wellness plans, as well as university work." It's your turn. Who could serve as your commitment partner and what would you ask of that person?

My commitment partner is	
I need the following from this person:	
We will check in	☐ Daily ☐ Two times per week ☐ Three times per week ☐ Weekly ☐ Biweekly

The last area we'd like to focus on, in terms of taking care of yourself, is compassion fatigue. Most of the time, faculty experience compassion satisfaction, which is the pleasure we derive from being able to do our work well (Stamm, 2010). When we feel effective, especially when we see evidence of our students' learning or publications being accepted, our compassion satisfaction increases and we enjoy our work.

COMPASSION FATIGUE IS A COMBINATION OF PHYSICAL, EMOTIONAL, AND SPIRITUAL DEPLETION ASSOCIATED WITH THE WORK WE DO WITH OTHERS.

The other side of this coin is compassion fatigue. Compassion fatigue is a combination of physical, emotional, and spiritual depletion associated with the trauma-related work we do where others are in significant emotional pain or physical distress. It's known as the high cost of caring. As Figley (2002) notes, "Compassion fatigue is a state experienced by those helping people in distress; it is an extreme state of tension and preoccupation with the suffering of those being helped to the degree that it can create a secondary traumatic stress for the helper" (p. 1435). As Elliott, Elliott, and Spears (2018) note,

> Symptoms can develop over a period of years, or after as little as six weeks on the job. Lowered tolerance for frustration, an aversion to working with certain students, and decreased job satisfaction are just a few of the effects that represent a significant risk to job performance as well as to teachers' own personal, emotional, and physical well-being. (p. 29)

The signs of compassion fatigue include

- Isolation

- Emotional outbursts

- Sadness, apathy

- Impulse to rescue anyone in need

- Persistent physical ailments

- Substance abuse

- Hypervigilance or hyperarousal

- Recurring nightmares or flashbacks

- Excessive complaints about colleagues, management, or those being helped

The American Academy of Family Physicians developed a self-assessment tool for health-care workers, which we have adapted for educators (see Figure 1.1). If you have these signs, please seek help. We need you. Your students need you. And compassion fatigue can be overcome.

Figure 1.1 Compassion Fatigue Inventory

Personal concerns commonly intrude on my professional role.	Yes	No
My colleagues seem to lack understanding.	Yes	No
I find even small changes enormously draining.	Yes	No
I can't seem to recover quickly after association with trauma.	Yes	No
Association with trauma affects me very deeply.	Yes	No
My students' stress affects me deeply.	Yes	No
I have lost my sense of hopefulness.	Yes	No
I feel vulnerable all the time.	Yes	No
I feel overwhelmed by unfinished personal business.	Yes	No

Source: Used with permission from Overcoming Compassion Fatigue, Apr. 2000, Vol. 7, No. 4, *Family Practice Management.* Copyright © 2000 American Academy of Family Physicians. All rights reserved.

CONCLUSION

We started with a recommendation to take care of yourself. We hope you take this seriously and carefully consider actions you can take. We promise that the rest of the book focuses on teaching and learning in distance learning using the knowledge gained from the Visible Learning database. As a final task for this module, now that you have a sense of what might be involved in taking care of yourself, complete the self-assessment on the following page.

FACTOR	USING THE "TRAFFIC LIGHT" SCALE, EVALUATE YOUR CURRENT LEVEL OF IMPLEMENTATION (GREEN IS GOOD OR REGULARLY; RED IS THE OPPOSITE).	USING THE SCALE BELOW, DETERMINE HOW IMPORTANT THIS FACTOR IS FOR YOU.
Recognizing trauma		not at all somewhat very extremely
Creating a workspace		not at all somewhat very extremely
Establishing personal routines		not at all somewhat very extremely
Socializing with others		not at all somewhat very extremely
Managing stress		not at all somewhat very extremely
Eating and sleeping well		not at all somewhat very extremely
Exercising		not at all somewhat very extremely
Finding a commitment partner		not at all somewhat very extremely
Recognizing compassion fatigue		not at all somewhat very extremely

MODULE 2

THE FIRST WEEK OF CLASSES

The first week of classes for students and faculty is no different than the first day of school for college and university students and colleagues. The night before the first week of classes for students is usually fraught with a mixture of anticipation and anxiety. For first-year students or freshmen, will I know anyone in my classes? How difficult are my classes going to be? For those starting their major courses, did I really pick the right major? Have I met all of my requirements for my general education requirement? What will my capstone or thesis project be? Oh, and regardless of the age, everyone still worries about what they will wear. As faculty, we have similar concerns. How will we relate to this semester's cohort? Will these students engage in the course content? How are the first-years or freshmen adjusting? From both sides of the podium, both want to make good impressions, and this brings anticipation and anxiety.

Whether in a distance learning environment or a face-to-face one, starting off the semester on the right foot matters. As Mary Poppins says, "Well begun is half done." Consider your typical rituals for the first week of classes or even the very first class of the semester. Do you make sure you are greeting students at the door? Have you adjusted the classroom so that it has been customized for them (e.g., a circle for discussion, pods for collaborative learning)? Do you have name cards for them to use at their seat? Do you have poster paper and markers ready for use? Are there organizational systems for students to submit problem sets, reading reflections, papers, or laboratory reports? A distance learning classroom needs precisely the same structures, albeit in a virtual space.

DRAWING ON MY EXPERTISE

What are the five top goals you want to achieve during your class meeting or first week of classes? Don't worry about the environment. Focus on your major goals (e.g., get to know something about each student's interests, establish norms and procedures, engage them in foundational content related to the course). You'll refer back to these goals at the end of the module.

1. _____

_____

2. _____

_____

3. _____

_____

4. _____

_____

5. _____

_____

DEVELOP A CLASSROOM MANAGEMENT PLAN FOR DISTANCE LEARNING

A virtual/distance classroom management plan is a faculty-created document that captures the norms, agreements, procedures, and schedules that will be used. Experienced faculty members may long ago have internalized their classroom management plan, but a distance learning environment requires some rethinking about what works well for you and your students. Committing a thoughtful and well-constructed plan to paper is a first step in a proactive approach to distance learning and can prevent problems from emerging. It can also be a tool for you to decide in advance of a situation how you will respond. Being proactive, not reactive, is key to good classroom management. Classrooms without a classwide approach to learning have more instances of negative student–teacher interactions and less time spent on academic instruction (Conroy, Sutherland, Snyder, & Marsh, 2008).

It is useful to understand the difference between classroom management and behavior management. For the most part, behavior management is a challenge we dodge in postsecondary teaching with the exception of appropriate student–student interaction. However, managing a learning environment (classroom management) is just as relevant for us as it is for our college colleagues. How often have we received emails, office hours visits, and comments on our course evaluations expressing frustration about procedures and schedules? How to submit work? When particular assignments or tasks are due? A classroom management plan outlines the necessary procedures, routines, and expectations for all the students in the class. These include simple routines such as submitting work, making revisions to work, retrieving materials or resources on reserve, as well as more conceptual ideas such as the expectations about the way students interact with others and their learning environment like engaging in classroom discussion or working on collaborative projects. On the other hand, discipline, or behavior management, is a component of the overall classroom management plan and is devoted to how problem behavior is prevented, as well as the approach one will use in addressing problem behavior. For example, do we have a plan for ensuring that student-to-student interactions are positive, inclusive, and culturally responsive?

Shannon Michelson is a sociology professor who uses driving questions to foster academic discourse in her criminology course. "When I first initiate a small group discussion, I provide clear guidelines for student etiquette in those discussions. For example, if I pose the question, 'Do we, as a capitalist society, need deviant behavior? Does it serve a function in our society?' I share a list of norms that help prevent problem behavior and establish norms of the group."

BREAKOUT ROOM NORMS

1. Mute yourself if you are not speaking.

2. Keep your camera on and look into the camera.

3. Be mindful of your background and what might appear in that background.

4. Keep things done in private, private.

5. Do not multitask—be present.

6. Only chat to the entire room—no private chatting.

7. If you would like to use the chat box, remember that this is public and a record of the chat is kept and archived.

8. Do not speak in generalities; recognize that your perspective is your perspective and may not be the perspective of others.

9. Maintain respect at all times in speaking, writing, and appearance.

To begin developing a classroom management plan for distance learning, start with a statement of your teaching and learning philosophy. What are your views and beliefs about how teaching and learning should occur in your distance classroom? What are your beliefs concerning community and diversity? Your statement should be no more than a few sentences long, yet be clear enough for your department head and students to understand your teaching philosophy. Focusing first on your beliefs about teaching and learning is significant in that who you are as a teacher drives the plan. Teresa Harrison in the department of writing and rhetoric emphasizes that writing is an iterative process. Therefore, she shares that, "Learning in WRTC 211 is best done in an environment that promotes the continuous edit and revising of our work based on the exchange of ideas through academic discourse and feedback." This philosophical statement paves the way for her to proactively establish norms, procedures, routines, and expectations for all the students in the class.

Keep your audiences in mind—if you are teaching a general education section of a course versus an upper-level majors section, we will need differing levels of management. For example, in an upper-level majors section, students are well into their program of study and have quite likely embraced the disciplinary processes and practices. However, in a general education course, learners are quite likely just learning about disciplinary processes and practices. Again, the distance learning classroom management plan will look different.

Once the classroom management plan has been constructed, share this plan with your students. Post this on your learning management system (LMS) and share it digitally through your initial communication with the students. This is recommended for two reasons: It serves as an initial means for welcoming students at the beginning of the semester, and it can become a tool for discussion when a difficulty does arise with a specific student. This module will address many of the aspects of a sound distance classroom management plan.

BEING PROACTIVE, NOT REACTIVE, IS KEY TO GOOD CLASSROOM MANAGEMENT.

NOTE TO SELF

What is your philosophy of teaching and learning in a distance space? Write no more than 100 words to craft a succinct message.

Figure 2.1 Peer-to-Peer Learning Norms

Source: Courtesy of Annie Warnimont and Jackie Foran, Nova Southeastern University Florida.

ESTABLISH NORMS

Groups of people interact according to the norms that have been agreed upon. The interesting thing is that groups will adopt their own norms whether they are formally named or not. You've witnessed this phenomenon countless times when you have met an established group for the first time. You may wonder why that group of old college buddies continuously insults each other or be struck by how solicitous and polite your friend's family gatherings are. Unstated norms in the virtual/distance classroom will evolve, for better or worse.

Norms govern how individuals in the group interact with one another and delineate what will be tolerated and what will not. Note how your interactions change depending on the group you are in. Your behavior is shaped in part by what the group expects of you, whether it is a gathering of neighbors, attendees of a religious organization, or a professional learning community. The norms of the classroom are the beliefs and values you want the collective classroom community to abide by. As any experienced faculty member knows, formally stated norms become a handy tool to refer to at the beginning of a class, or when problems arise.

A major learning many experienced in the rapid conversion to distance learning in 2020 is that the norms of the classroom were forgotten. Whether face-to-face instruction preceded distance learning, or whether you are meeting students for the first time, consider the norms you want your students and yourself to embody. One example of a distance classroom's norms can be found in Figure 2.1. These were developed as a way to establish the norms that govern their peer-to-peer learning, at a distance.

NOTE TO SELF

What are the norms you want your students to use as they interact with one another and with you in distance learning? We ask some questions to spark your thinking, although not all of them may apply to your class.

- What habits and dispositions are needed to be successful learners?

- What should they learn about themselves as learners?

- How should they interact with you and others to maintain learning conditions?

- What should they do with their learning?

LINK NORMS TO CLASS AGREEMENTS

The norms you create for your distance classroom space become the foundation for the agreements you want to use. These agreements are an essential component for managing a smooth-running learning environment. Well-crafted agreements communicate the teacher's expectations for the class as it relates to climate and student performance. It is important to note that once created, agreements must be explicitly taught to students. To be very honest, putting norms in the syllabus does not lead to agreements in your class. During the first week of classes, we have to revisit and apply these norms or agreements to specific learning tasks. This discussion, modeling, and demonstrating of norms will ensure that these expectations become the norm in how students work together in the class. New technologies further increase the need for rules in digital environments. The use of discussion boards and online collaborative tools has increased the need to ensure that students are taught the norms and expectations of how they work together (Staarman, 2009).

Mark Laumakis (San Diego State University, Psychology) shares how he sets norms and routines.

resources.corwin.com/ DLPlaybook-college

You'll notice that we call them *agreements* rather than *rules*. We do so because agreements represent the social contract of the classroom community, rather than a narrower set of behavioral guidelines that have been written by the teacher alone. A review of fifteen studies on the characteristics of these agreements confirmed what many teachers already know (Alter & Haydon, 2017):

- **A fewer number, rather than more, works better.** The recommendation is about three to five.

- **Co-construct them with students.** That's why we call them agreements. Even young students have a good sense of what is right and fair.

- **State them positively.** Beware of a list of agreements that all begin with the word *No* because these do not tell students what they should do, only what they should not. Behavior cannot exist in a vacuum, and in the absence of clear statements, students are left to speculate about what is acceptable.

- **Make them specific in nature.** Agreements that are specific in nature state explicitly what the expected behavior should be, which is a key to building students' ability to self-regulate.

- **Post the agreements.** Once developed, they should be clearly posted in your distance classroom. One way to do so is to put them on a chart that is behind your head so that students can see them. Another advantage is that you can refer directly to the agreement when redirecting a student's problem behavior.

- **Teach and rehearse the expectations.** This is a critical component for ensuring an efficient distance classroom. The agreements should be taught during each distance learning session during the first week of classes and revisited occasionally throughout the remainder of the semester, especially after fall break. The faculty member should model each agreement so that students can learn what they look and sound like. For example, if one of the agreements is about written communication on discussion boards, model examples of how these are done in ways that are respectful and academically appropriate.

Kara Ford, a professor of social work, uses the first day of class and the first small group discussion to co-construct agreements in her Human Behavior in the Social Environment course. "The very nature of this course evokes passionate class discussions. Rather than me listing off dos and don'ts, their first small group task is to establish norms and a plan for enforcing those norms. I send them into breakout rooms and tell them they have 10 minutes to get this set up." The seemingly restrictive time limit forces Dr. Ford's students to get right to work. "They always rise to the challenge and develop agreements that include [the following]:

- Be respectful of each other's perspectives by acknowledging that the perspective has value regardless of whether we agree with that perspective.

- Using clarifying and probing questions to gain understanding rather than make assumptions.

- Internally commit to making the group successful; be present and contribute.

These are so much better and they let students know what we expect, as a learning community, of each other."

Agreements serve to convey high expectations, mutual respect, and an acknowledgment of the learning community's needs. A set of rules that are strictly compliance based ("Don't speak unless called on.") tell the students that you're the one with all the power, and they better listen or else. We've actually seen this backfire on several occasions in distance learning classrooms. Faculty members who "mute" students for punitive purposes lose them emotionally and psychologically and encounter a lot of difficulty in reengaging at a distance. We've also heard of faculty who get angry with students for using the chat function in their distance classroom. If you don't want them to use the chat function, then set up your distance classroom with that feature turned off. Keep in mind, if you turn off the chat feature, they will just text each other. It's not fair to get mad at students. Providing ways for them to use the chat function in respectful ways is far more useful anyway.

Agreements that emphasize a collaborative spirit ("Listen and respond respectfully, even when you disagree.") signal students that learning is social and done in the company of others. It also lets students know that your role is to foster learning. After all, they are adults and are mere steps away from entering the workforce or postbaccalaureate education. Just to be clear, you may be thinking that classroom agreements are necessary only for PreK—12 learners, but the evidence is to the contrary. One example is a study of undergraduates enrolled in a human resource development program that shows well-developed agreements contribute positively to peer—peer relationships and increase participation of students in distance learning teams (e.g., Johnson, Suriya, Yoon, Berrett, & La Fleur, 2002).

UNSTATED NORMS IN THE VIRTUAL/ DISTANCE CLASSROOM WILL EVOLVE, FOR BETTER OR WORSE.

NOTE TO SELF

Revisit the norms you developed in the previous section. What are the three to five agreements you want to co-construct with your students?

1. _____

   _____

   _____

2. _____

   _____

   _____

3. _____

   _____

   _____

4. _____

   _____

   _____

5. _____

   _____

   _____

IDENTIFY EXPECTATIONS FOR SYNCHRONOUS DISTANCE LEARNING

Teaching at a distance poses some unique challenges that we never confront in face-to-face teaching. Distance learning is usually a combination of synchronous and asynchronous experiences, and each poses unique challenges. Let's start with synchronous learning. One expectation we had to confront early on when we rapidly switched to distance learning concerned the issue of cameras. Some students turned them on; most of the students did not (e.g., 8:00 a.m., Monday morning classes). This initially seemed like a no-brainer—of course they should have them on! After all, could you even imagine teaching in a face-to-face class where everyone had a blanket over their heads? To be sure, we rely on being able to read students' facial expressions and body language so that we can teach responsively.

But in talking with faculty and students, we realized the issue of laptop cameras is more complicated. For instance, what about students who are Muslim, and girls and women don't wear the hijab in their own homes. In households that are short on space, asking female family members to cover during their children's online learning seems burdensome. There are also students who don't want to show their homes to others for any number of reasons. These are sensitive topics that require sensitive approaches. Here's where we have landed. We ask students to either turn on their camera or use a picture so that they are easily recognizable to others. And when they are in breakout rooms, most of the students turn their cameras on so that they can see others. We also learned that teaching them to hide the self-view resulted in an increase in the use of cameras. As Mateo, a student of political science, said, "I don't like looking at myself for the whole class. When I learned how to turn off the self-view, I didn't mind having the camera on."

We have also added other possible expectations to use with students when it comes to synchronous learning.

FOR YOUR CONSIDERATION

How will your students learn about your synchronous distance classroom? Here are some suggested items to address specific questions students are likely to have.

Getting Ready for Your Class Meeting

- Make sure you have completed the pre-class preparation activity so that you'll be ready to learn!
- Think about your goals for learning today. What do you want to achieve?
- Work with your family to find a quiet space that won't disturb other people in your house and won't distract you from learning.
- Prepare your learning space. Make sure you have a clear workspace to write and store your materials.
- If there are items that have personal information you wouldn't want other people to see, move them out of camera range.
- Check your lighting so that your classmates can see you.
- Check to see that your first and last names are on the screen.

(Continued)

(Continued)

During Class Meetings

- Ask clarifying questions so you fully understand the learning intentions and success criteria for this particular class meeting.
- Listen carefully to others and ask good questions!
- Use the reaction buttons to let your classmates know when you agree or disagree and give them a thumbs-up or a round of applause to encourage them.
- The hand raising button helps all of us know when you've got something important to say.
- When you are not speaking, mute your microphone. It helps other people hear.
- Turn off notifications from email and social media so you aren't distracted.
- If you have a smartphone, shut it down so you aren't distracted.

At the Close of the Class Meeting

- Review the goals you set for today. Did you achieve them?
- Ask clarifying questions so you fully understand the learning intentions and success criteria for the lesson. Did you achieve the learning intentions and success criteria? How do you know?
- Make sure you know how to access assigned learning tasks to prepare for the next meeting.

DEVELOP AND TEACH ORGANIZATIONAL AND PROCEDURAL ROUTINES

Another element of your distance classroom management plan concerns the procedures and organizational structures needed to ensure learning takes place. Although the environment may be different, many of the same organizational requirements remain the same.

1. **Provide a clear schedule in your syllabus so students can organize resources.** From here on out, chances are good that students will have more than one distance learning situation. Juggling the online schedules of four or five classes can be challenging for even the most organized student. Providing a clear schedule allows students to organize their time around the other responsibilities they may have as a result of remote learning.

   - Build weekly and semester-long schedules and show students where to find them on your LMS.

   - These schedules provide information about when specific tasks and resources will be available on your LMS. For example, when will certain modules be available and unavailable during the week or semester?

2. **Furnish your daily and or weekly schedule at the beginning of the semester.** Learning intentions and success criteria are crucial for learning, and we will address those in more detail in Module 6. Providing your schedule to the learners helps them know when you will and won't be available to answer questions or provide assistance. This is analogous to posting our office hours outside of our office doors.

   - The schedule should list time slots for distance office hours.
   - The consistent availability for distance office hours establishes a predictable learning environment and assists learners in pacing their rate of work.

3. **Teach students the signals you will use.** Faculty need a signal to gain the attention of students at the beginning of class, when students are engaged in dialogue with peers, or when transitioning from one activity to another.

   - The signals should be taught daily during the first week of classes and reinforced frequently until students respond quickly and consistently.

   - The use of a signal to gain attention promotes student engagement by minimizing the amount of lost instructional time.

   - Use an online elapsed timer display when setting up tasks students will be completing in real time. This further signals to students how to best use their remaining time to complete independent work such as reflective writing.

   - Many distance classroom platforms feature elapsed timers for small group breakout rooms. Make sure students are aware of these features so that they can monitor their use of time in peer-to-peer small group learning.

4. **Create procedures for how students will retrieve materials.** Few things are more frustrating than trying to figure out where to find materials for online classes.

   - Clearly label digital folders by date and topic so that students can easily locate them.

   - Identify which need to be printed in advance for an online activity. You will want to keep these to an absolute minimum as they can create a burden for students who do not have access to a campus computing center or printing station. Having said that, if there is something that students need to print, name it.

5. **Create procedures for how students will submit assignments**. Over the course of the semester, students will turn in a large number of assignments. Invariably, some of these documents will lack important information such as a name or date. Grading is further complicated when the topic of the assignment is unclear. With the advent of digital resources, the naming of documents holds similar problems. It is difficult

to process and locate 100 assignments that are all unhelpfully named "HIST 101 Term Paper."

- Teach students a system for heading their assignments at the beginning of the year to make recordkeeping easier.
- Be sure to instruct them on properly naming the file so that you (and they) can locate it quickly. The title of the document should contain the student's last name, the name of the course, and a one- or two-word description.

Heading Requirements	Example	Nonexample
First and last name	Gavin Maxwell	GM
Date	4/18/21 or April 18, 2021	April
Class/Section	HIST 101, Section 3	history
Assignment	Primary Document Analysis	questions

File-Saving Requirements	Example	Nonexample
Last name	Maxwell	GMax
Class/Section	HIST101_3	history
Assignment	PDAnalysis	Assign1
Extension	.doc	Left blank

DESIGN A CONSIDERATE WEBSITE

Alex Gonzalez (San Diego State University, Educational Leadership) talks about introducing the learning management system.

resources.corwin.com/ DLPlaybook-college

Colleges and universities routinely purchase licenses for a single platform that all faculty are expected to use. Website design has advanced considerably since the early days of the World Wide Web. Most of us have been on websites that were distracting or unhelpful. This has, in part, led to the requirement that all of PreK–16 include universal design principles to make website usage easier. This has been influenced in part by Section 508 of the Rehabilitation Act of 1998 that requires federal agencies and their affiliates to make websites accessible to people with disabilities. These requirements are beneficial for all users. The Web Content Accessibility Guidelines 2.0 is available at https://www.w3.org/TR/WCAG20/. They recommend that websites be

- **Perceivable:** Use color, background, and size of text judiciously to ensure that the information can be viewed.

- **Operable:** Make sure that the information can be driven by the keyboard and that anything timed for display (such as Flash animation) can be adjusted for speed.

- **Understandable:** Use appropriate text language and avoid placing too much text, or text that is too long, on a single page.

- **Robust:** The information should be useful and compatible with other technologies.

Most LMS platforms have been designed to address many of these issues. Be sure to consult your Instructional Technology department for specific requirements. Consider three distinct places that will be highly useful to students:

THE LANDING PAGE

- The home page should contain the most frequently requested information, including
  - Your contact information (email, Twitter handle, and phone number other than your office)
  - A description of the course or class and a navigation bar for the other pages

- Also remember:
  - While the home page should be visually interesting, it should not be cluttered.
  - Avoid using distracting backgrounds that make it difficult to read.
  - Create a link to your email address so that students can readily contact you.

THE STUDENT PAGE

- This is the ideal place for your syllabus and classroom management plan, as well as a current list of assignments and projects. Nothing looks more dated than a website that features assignments that were due months ago.

- In some cases, you may also post handouts (e.g., slide decks, links to videos, links to log-in pages for internet resources) and other materials.

- Consider featuring a reminder for students to contact you with questions, and update this information regularly so you can respond in a timely manner.

NOTE TO SELF

Students retrieve information at any time of the day or week. Develop an FAQ (frequently asked questions) to post on your student pages.

QUESTIONS	YOUR RESPONSES
Where can I find weekly and monthly schedules?	
Where do I find assignments and materials?	
How do I submit work?	
How do I retrieve graded work?	
How do I contact the teacher for academic help?	
How do I get technical help?	

YOUR FIRST DISTANCE CLASSES

Now, it's time to teach! All of this careful planning is about to pay off. If this is the first time you have interacted with the specific students in your class, getting to know your students is the first order of business, whether in a face-to-face or distance learning environment. Students are also new to each other and need lots of opportunities to learn about one another. If these are students that are in the major and you know them from another course, advising, or as teaching and laboratory assistants, catching up on how they are doing should be the first order of business.

GREET STUDENTS

Could you imagine not greeting the people you live with when they return home for the day? We never think to ourselves, "I said hello to my son yesterday, so I really don't need to do it today." Yet in the busy flow of the semester, this is exactly what can happen. We've noticed that is one of the first routines that deteriorates after the first few weeks of the semester. Even if it is the week before finals, students deserve to be greeted by name. If it means logging into the distance classroom fifteen minutes earlier to set up your distance classroom (e.g., background, materials), please do so. Be ready for them as they sign into that class and say hello, use their name, and look them in the eyes. Be the first one there!

David Reynolds, a biology professor, not only greets his learners but gives them a do-now task that gives him a quick read on how they are doing and if they are ready to learn. "I start most classes with an image or meme that relates to the topic of the class. My learners are tasked with developing a caption for that meme that weaves together the readings for the week or the concepts we are focusing on in class."

Josh Streeter (James Madison University, Theater and Dance) shares how to start strong on the first class meeting.

resources.corwin.com/ DLPlaybook-college

PERSONALIZE THE SPACE

A distance classroom community is one that shares a common space. Add details so that students see themselves and their unique contributions. For example, have learners share their reading reflections, worked problems, Exegesis, or artwork as part of the focus for the learning. Students should be encouraged to create their own virtual backgrounds that reflect their identity or how they are making meaning of the learning. For example, Kerry Crenshaw asked her molecular biology students to develop thinking maps related to outside reading assignments. "I asked my students to make their thinking maps their virtual backgrounds and then allowed them to ask each other probing or clarify questions about how they arranged the concepts and ideas."

LEARN STUDENTS' NAMES AND HOW TO PRONOUNCE THEM

Addressing people by name is a fundamental signal of respect. When we take the time to learn other people's names, we indicate our interest in them. Hearing our own name spoken by another alerts our attention and creates an emotional link to the person saying our name. A challenge for faculty that may see their students once a week is in learning their names and pronouncing them correctly. Some names are more familiar than others, depending on the faculty member's own experiences. But as anyone who has a difficult name can attest, hearing your name said incorrectly can be discouraging. Creative ways of learning students' names afford opportunities to learn more about their lives and their personalities. Saying a student's name correctly is "a powerful fulcrum for harnessing student engagement and motivation in a classroom" (Elwell & Lopez Elwell, 2020, p. 13). Not knowing or being unwilling to use a student's name contributes negatively to a sense of "otherness" and a belief that the student is not valued in the classroom.

Go deeper with students by learning about the story behind their name. We tell stories about how we got our names, which invites a bit of family lore into the classroom and lets students ponder the seemingly impossible notion that once we were babies ourselves. After modeling, we ask students to tell or write about how they got their names. Some may talk about being named after an ancestor or family friend, while others may offer the translated meaning of their name. As they tell the story of their name, we ask them about their preferred names, and if we aren't adept at pronouncing it correctly, we ask them to coach us. Doug asks his students not to let him off the hook and practices each day with them until he is able to say it correctly.

IT IS USEFUL TO PROBE STUDENTS' INTERESTS AT VARIOUS POINTS THROUGHOUT THE SEMESTER, NOT ONLY DURING THE FIRST WEEK OF CLASSES.

SILENT INTERVIEW

We have used a silent interview with students to introduce one another to the class. Students interview one another in pairs by writing questions on a collaborative document. The pairs then answer their partner's questions. After about ten minutes, the students introduce their partner to the rest of the class.

Another technique for students is to invite them to write a short essay about themselves, including such details as their character traits, aspirations, and biography. Students then convert their essay into a word cloud, choosing fonts, colors, and designs that are pleasing to them. After sharing information about themselves to the class, they can be displayed virtually using the learning management system for the class. Make sure you participate, too, so that your students can learn about you. Encourage students to use these as their virtual backgrounds during the first week of classes.

NOTE TO SELF

What routines will you use during the first week of classes to learn your students' names and the stories behind them?

LEARN STUDENTS' INTERESTS

Interest is a key lever for building relevancy into learning, as students with a higher degree of interest in a topic are more likely to perform at higher levels (Palmer, Dixon, & Archer, 2016). Having said that, "interest" isn't likely to manifest itself as a purely academic pursuit. We can't imagine a student breathlessly saying, "I can't wait to learn about the failed Gunpowder Plot of 1604!" But she may be interested in social change, and protests may be a hook for her. She might even be interested in knowing about Guy Fawkes, the leader of the Gunpowder Plot, and the mask that is often worn to disguise the identity of contemporary protesters.

Interest is not static. It is situational and multidimensional across several constructs from low to high. Issues such as its value, frequency, and mastery shift over time, as virtually any faculty member can attest. Topics that a student found absorbing at the beginning of the year may suddenly become boring, while a new interest may replace it. After all, how many times have your students changed the topic of their capstone projects or thesis?

With remote learning, we may find it easier to simply go through the motions as the semester goes on. We get tired and our schedules fill up with meetings and other obligations as faculty members. As the semester goes on, we begin to simply log in, run our classes, and then log out. Therefore, we begin to lose

THERE IS A TREMENDOUS OPPORTUNITY TO FORGE A POSITIVE TEACHER–STUDENT RELATIONSHIP BY TELLING A STUDENT, "I READ THIS AND I THOUGHT OF YOU."

contact and connection with our students. As we said before, our learners are also getting into disciplinary content, processes, and practices that will likely have an impact on their interests. We don't want to miss the opportunity to mentor them through this process. As students have more and more experiences in different disciplines, it is useful to probe students' interests at various points throughout the semester, not only during the first week of classes.

One way to probe students' interests at various points throughout the semester is to develop tasks that are due at various points during the semester and offer learners choices based on their own interests. Scott Polumbo, physics professor, has three choice-based assignments built into his modern physics course. These assignments are spaced out so that he can probe his students' interests beyond the first week of classes. "First, I ask them to select an article in an area of modern physics that interests them and conduct peer review of the article as if they were reviewing it. Then, they have to set up time during office hours to talk through their review. I get to ask them questions about why they selected the article and better understand what area of physics most captures their attention."

Dr. Polumbo also has his students replicate one of the key experiments in modern physics and, at the end of the semester, present their response to the question, What does an atom really look like? "These three assignments are really open ended and allow me to engage in dialogue about ideas in physics and why the individual student finds these ideas to be so interesting. Their own interests in the field come up every time, without fail. I think the most important part about these assignments is that I get to converse with my students, even if it is through a computer, and hear why they chose what they did for each of these assignments. The grade really doesn't matter to me."

NOTE TO SELF

Knowing about your students' interests is a key lever for building relevancy into your teaching. How will you learn about them? Identify useful approaches to learning about your students' interests throughout the semester.

CONCLUSION

The first class meeting with distance instruction, whether it occurs at the beginning of the semester or intermittently throughout the semester, demands careful attention. If you have the opportunity to initially teach students in a face-to-face classroom, make the most of it by getting them ready for a period of distance learning. Begin by returning to the five goals you identified at the beginning of this module and use them to foreground your developing plans. Make revisions as needed to align your goals with your plans for implementation. As a final task for this module, complete the following self-assessment so that you can identify where to target your efforts.

FACTOR	USING THE "TRAFFIC LIGHT" SCALE, EVALUATE YOUR CURRENT LEVEL OF IMPLEMENTATION (GREEN IS GOOD OR REGULARLY; RED IS THE OPPOSITE).	USING THE SCALE BELOW, DETERMINE HOW IMPORTANT THIS FACTOR IS FOR YOU.
Establishing norms		not at all · somewhat · very · extremely
Linking norms to class agreements		not at all · somewhat · very · extremely
Identifying expectations for synchronous distance learning		not at all · somewhat · very · extremely
Developing and teaching organizational and procedural routines		not at all · somewhat · very · extremely
Designing a considerate website		not at all · somewhat · very · extremely
Greeting students		not at all · somewhat · very · extremely
Learning students' names and how to pronounce them		not at all · somewhat · very · extremely
Learning students' interests		not at all · somewhat · very · extremely

MODULE 3

FACULTY–STUDENT RELATIONSHIPS FROM A DISTANCE

LEARNING INTENTIONS

- I am learning about the value of student–faculty relationships and the maintenance of those relationships in distance learning.

- I am learning about my role in creating an environment in which students feel comfortable to make errors.

- I am learning about the design of distance learning experiences.

SUCCESS CRITERIA

- I can describe the characteristics of valuable faculty–student relationships.

- I can use the elements of faculty–student relationships (teacher empathy, unconditional positive regard, genuineness, nondirectivity, and encouragement of critical thinking) in my interactions with students.

- I leverage my relationships to create an environment in which errors are valued.

- I recognize the signs of a chilly classroom and work to avoid that feeling.

- I redouble my efforts to reach hard-to-teach students.

- I can design systems that increase touchpoints for students virtually.

Ask a faculty member what matters in learning and within moments they will be talking about the human connection. For many of us, we immediately talk about working alongside an undergraduate as they work through an organic chemistry experiment, teach their first lesson to a room full of students, develop the first draft of a piece of writing, or prepare their first tax return. Knowing one's students as individuals with rich stories to tell and aspirations for their futures is an essential disposition for us as mentors, advisors, and teachers at postsecondary institutions. What do you remember about your professors during your undergraduate years or graduate years? Who did you learn best from? Likely it was a faculty member with whom you had a positive relationship. This faculty member may or may not have been your advisor, but you developed a positive relationship with this individual and the relationship evolved into an apprenticeship-like model of learning. Positive relationships between faculty members and their students form the heart of what Hattie and Zierer (2018) refer to as the mindframes of Visible Learning or ways of thinking about teaching and learning:

1. I focus on learning and the language of learning. Rather than passing a competency-based exam, earning licensure in a field, or getting into law school or medical school, do you focus solely on your students' learning? Are the conversations you have with your students focused on learning disciplinary content, processes, and practices?

2. I strive for challenge and not merely "doing your best." Moving beyond placing narrated slide decks online and claiming that is the best I can do now is very different than looking at this as an opportunity to reframe our class experiences. Do you embrace the challenge?

3. I recognize that learning is hard work. Although we know this in our own academic pursuits, we now find ourselves learning about teaching from a distance. Do you acknowledge that this is hard work?

4. I build relationships and trust so that learning can occur in a place where it is safe to make mistakes and learn from others. Just because our students are watching a computer screen, the desire to connect is still there. How do we extend the mentoring and advising beyond the walls of the classroom?

5. I engage as much in dialogue as monologue. Sit and get does not work. How do you capitalize on tools and technology to dialogue with students and colleagues?

6. I inform all about the language of learning. As academics, we can easily find ourselves in a bubble. In what ways do you talk about learning in the new normal?

7. I am a change agent and believe that all students can improve. At the end of the day we have to believe that we have the capacity to create a learning experience, whether face-to-face or remotely, that moves student learning forward. This particular mindframe should be leveraged to improve teaching in distance environments and improve our readiness, as well as our students' capacity, to continue their postsecondary education regardless of the setting.

8. I give and help students to understand feedback and I interpret and act on feedback given to me. As we will share in an upcoming module, feedback is necessary to close the gap between where are students are and where they are going in their learning. From a distance, this requires the intentional planning of when and how to deliver that feedback. Furthermore, we have to listen to our students and recognize that they will give us feedback on how things are going. We must act on that feedback.

9. I see assessment as informing my impact and next steps. We maximize learning when both us and our students understand the results of assessments and use the results to take action on future teaching and learning. Do your assessments help you make decisions about the next class meeting?

10. I collaborate with other teachers. This mindframe will come up over and over again. We cannot go at this alone. Our success and fulfilling the hope that those of us that have always engaged in teaching and learning on campus will return better than before hinges on collective efforts of all of us. Do you seek opportunities to collaborate for better teaching and learning outcomes?

Consider the extent to which the quality of the relationship between educator and learner underpins many of these mindframes. There is the social sensitivity needed to understand that learning is hard work and to never demean students' efforts. The orientation to dialogic, rather than monologic, teaching suggests that the teacher takes students' ideas seriously and allows them to hear how and what students are thinking or processing. These teachers know that feedback is about what is received, not only what is given, and that a fraught relationship diminishes feedback's usefulness. Teachers hold dear to a core assumption: They deeply believe that they can change the trajectory of a child's educational path and have evidence of their impact to do so.

So, what are the characteristics for a high-quality teacher–student relationship? Before we delve more deeply into that topic, we invite you to reflect on your experiences.

DRAWING ON MY EXPERTISE

What are the three to five quality indicators you use to judge whether a relationship with a student is a positive and productive one?

1. _____

_____

2. _____

_____

3. _____

_____

4. _____

_____

5. _____

CHARACTERISTICS OF FACULTY-STUDENT RELATIONSHIPS

People learn better when they have a positive relationship with the person providing instruction. The evidence of the influence of teacher–student relationships is a positive one, with an effect size of 0.48 (Hattie, 2018). The story behind the data speaks to its potential to accelerate achievement. Elements of teacher–student relationships (Cornelius-White, 2007, p. 113) include

- **Teacher empathy**—understanding
- **Unconditional positive regard**—warmth
- **Genuineness**—the teacher's self-awareness
- **Nondirectivity**—student-initiated and student-regulated activities
- **Encouragement of critical thinking** as opposed to traditional memory emphasis

These student-centered practices are essential in any classroom, perhaps even more so in a distance one. Establishing these conditions begins from the first interactions students have with the teacher:

- Strong faculty–student relationships rely on effective communication and a willingness to address issues that strain the relationship.

- Positive relationships are fostered and maintained when faculty set fair expectations, involve students in determining aspects of the classroom organization and management, and hold students accountable for the expectations in an equitable way.

- Importantly, relationships are not destroyed when problematic behaviors occur, on the part of either us or our students. This is an important point for faculty. If we want to ensure students read, write, communicate, and think at high levels, we have to develop positive, trusting relationships with *each* student.

As important, high levels of positive relationships build trust and make your classroom a safe place to explore what students do not know, their errors, and misconceptions. Indeed, powerful faculty–student relationships allow errors to be seen as opportunities to learn. A lot of students (and professors) avoid situations where they are likely to make errors and feel challenged with exposing their lack of knowledge or understanding—but we want to turn these situations into powerful learning opportunities, and this is more likely to occur in high trust environments. And it is not just high positive levels of faculty–student relations, but how you develop high trust student–student relations so one student can talk about their struggles of learning with other students, and the notion of "struggle" becomes a positive and fun activity.

Gabriel Marcos, neurobiology professor, has the reputation among undergraduates, graduates, and colleagues for being a great teacher. Students take his neuroscience courses as electives. Yes, electives. When you speak with those students that are both neuroscience majors and those that stood in line to be granted overrides into the course, they all say the same thing. His students believe that they can and do learn from him. He has some of the highest ratings on campus. Interestingly students' rating of high-quality teaching has a good effect size at 0.45. Students know what good teaching is and are fairly accurate judges of whether or not they can learn from someone. When you ask Dr. Marcos why his students rate him so highly, he shyly responds,

Well, I think it's because I get to know them. I work on my relationship with each one of them. But I don't set out to be a friend. I set out to earn their trust so that they will take risks and make mistakes. For many students, they believe that neuroscience is simply learning about the parts of the brain. So once we move into concepts like resting potentials, threshold potentials, depolarization, and hyperpolarization, they have to trust me or there would be a stampede for the door before the drop/add date. When I earn this trust, that does not happen and I can push them; even those that are not neuroscience majors. I know that they'll learn more and value the experience. I will admit, it has been hard in distance learning to do

Hilary Campbell (Blue Ridge Community College, Psychology) discusses how she maintains a strong student–faculty relationship.

resources.corwin.com/ DLPlaybook-college

EVEN IF YOU HAVE HAD PREVIOUS FACE-TO-FACE INTERACTIONS WITH STUDENTS, DON'T NEGLECT REESTABLISHING RELATIONSHIPS WITH YOUR STUDENTS IN A VIRTUAL SPACE.

this, but I'm always thinking about how to make sure that students know I care and that they can trust me. I start every class meeting with a check-in so that they know that I'm there for them. And I talk about the mistakes I have made teaching online and how exciting it is to learn. In fact, I relate making mistakes to learning and the brain. They see me as human and are willing to make mistakes so that they can learn too.

Here's what is important to understand. Even if you have had previous face-to-face interactions with students before, don't neglect reestablishing your relationships with your students in a virtual space. When educators across the world had to rapidly shift from face-to-face to distance instruction in spring 2020, we were reminded of the fragile nature of relationships. We found ourselves needing to understand their students in new ways. We were suddenly exposed to our students' worlds as we saw into their homes. Likewise, they saw us in new ways. They study the pictures behind you on your living room wall and see your children interrupt your discussion on the supply and demand to ask for something to eat or to get assistance fetching a specific toy. Figuring out new parameters of an existing faculty–student relationship can be challenging to navigate. Your students count on you as a constant in their lives.

Dress professionally (you're still a teacher, even when you're teaching from home), show your enthusiasm for them and your work, and make sure that your warmth and regard for them is apparent.

JUDGMENT AND WILL, NOT JUST KNOWLEDGE AND ABILITY

Marva Cappello (San Diego State University, Education) shares the importance of mentoring teaching and graduate students.

resources.corwin.com/ DLPlaybook-college

The quality of a faculty–student relationship is dynamic, meaning that it is continually shaped by experiences and context. In the previous module, we shared ideas for ways to initiate relationships with new students, such as using one-on-one conferencing, study partners, or peer mentors to help them feel welcomed and to learn more about them. Utilizing these approaches is not the same as a relationship with students. These are simply activities that get you through the door with a student. The rest is up to you.

Narrow views of the teaching profession focus on knowledge and ability: Does a teacher know how to do _____ and have the ability to implement it? But when it comes to so many aspects of teaching and learning, it is really the teacher's *judgment* and *will* that truly matter (Zierer, Lachner, Tögel, & Weckend, 2018). We separate the "what" of teaching (knowledge and ability) from the "how" (will) and "why" (judgment) about what they do. Faculty–student relationships require not just an investment in fostering new ones ("what"), but in understanding the importance of building and maintaining them ("will") and the social sensitivity to sense when they will best serve the learner ("why").

How will you establish (or reestablish) relationships with students in a distance learning environment? We've started a list for you. How will you personalize it to your context?

Teacher Empathy How do students seek connections with you?	• Begin synchronous and asynchronous lessons with a positive affirmation (e.g., favorite quotes, a silly joke, short video messages). • Establish virtual office hours for students to drop in for academic support. • Host short check-in conferences with the student to see how they are doing and what they need. • •
Unconditional Positive Regard How will your students know you care about them as people?	• Weave into lessons what you have learned about students' pursuits and interests. • Provide polls for students to respond to at the end of class meetings. • Use voice feedback tools on student work so they can hear the sparkle in your voice, rather than read your words without context. • •
Genuineness How will your students know you care about yourself as a professional?	• Dress and groom professionally. • Project a demeanor that is optimistic about them and you. • Make it clear in words and actions that this is a place for learning about themselves, the world, and each other. • •
Nondirectivity How will your students know you hold their abilities in high regard?	• Hold individual conversations with students to help them identify their strengths, goals, and growth areas. • Ask questions that mediate the students' thinking, rather than asking leading questions. • Use shared decision-making about the learning progression of the class with students. • •
Encouragement of Critical Thinking	• Foster discussion among peers using questions that open up their thinking. • Every distance learning session includes opportunities for students to write about, illustrate, or discuss their thinking with peers. • Build choice and relevance into assignments and projects. • •

What are your "hows" and "whys" for faculty–student relationships in your practice?

How will you build and maintain relationships throughout the school year in a distance environment?	
Why are relationships central to your distance learning efforts?	

RELATIONSHIPS

PEER-TO-PEER RELATIONSHIPS ARE INFLUENCED, TOO

Faculty–student relationships influence peer perceptions of classmates. When a student asks a question indicating they are lost, do not know where they are going, or are just plain wrong, high levels of peer-to-peer relationships mean that this student is not ridiculed, does not feel that they should be silent and bear their not knowing alone, and can depend on the professor and often other students to help them out.

Unfortunately, in some cases, specific students are targeted for correction while other students engaged in the same behavior are not noticed. Given the number of back channels available for student communication, if we provide correction to one student in our classes, it is almost guaranteed that the other students will know about it. Aaron Botkin, an engineering professor, shared a story about peer-to-peer relationships. "I learned very quickly that the students start in my classes already having created a group text. They use this group text continuously to communicate about the class. If I respond to a student's email, I can almost guarantee that response is shared in the group text. At the same time, if I give different responses to different students, that is shared as well." Let's be clear. This level of communication can be positive. For example, if Dr. Botkin responds to a student's clarifying question in email, alerting the student that they should pass along the response is helpful. However, if a student is repeatedly provided feedback that is fundamentally different from other students, that will be passed along as well. The students will notice this inconsistency and likely interpret this as, "Dr. Botkin doesn't like Abby and wants her to drop this class." It's hard to develop positive relationships, and then achieve, when you feel unwanted. Being disliked by the teacher or peers has a negative influence on learning, with an effect size of –0.19 (Hattie, 2018). In fact, it is one of the few of 250-plus influences that actually *reverses* learning.

A PROFESSOR'S DISLIKE FOR A STUDENT IS RARELY A SECRET TO THEIR CLASSMATES.

A professor's dislike for a student is rarely a secret to classmates. Students are exquisitely attuned to the emotions of their professor. Think about it: They are observing you closely day after day, and they get very good at being able to read the social environment. They watch how you interact verbally and nonverbally with classmates. You are actually modeling how peers should interact with the specific student. Sadly, students who are disliked by us are more readily rejected by peers than those who are liked by the teacher (Birch & Ladd, 1997). This phenomenon, called *social referencing*, is especially influential among young children, who turn to adults to decide what they like and do not like. Elementary students are able to accurately state who is disliked by their teacher. In a study of 1,400 fifth graders, the students reported that they also did not like the children that the teachers told the researchers that they did not like. As the researchers noted, the "targeted" students were held in negative regard six months later, even though they were now in a new grade level with a different teacher (Hendrickx, Mainhard, Oudman, Boor-Klip, & Brekelmans, 2017). Much like a pebble dropped into a pond, being disliked by a teacher ripples across other social relationships and endures well beyond the time span of a negative interaction. Even though the research focuses on the PreK–12 classroom, there is no reason to believe that these findings cannot be extrapolated to our colleges and universities.

In a distance learning setting, your actions and nonverbal signals are right there for everyone to see and hear. You are on close-up and your reactions are noticeable. Everyone can see when you look away and stop listening to a student. They see when you have muted a classmate's microphone because he was asking questions that took the discussion off topic. Your negative relationship with a particular student can have two possible outcomes. The first is that peers take a dislike to the same student (a phenomenon that is especially true in the PreK–12). The second possible outcome is that they take a dislike to you. And a student who doesn't like you makes your job much more difficult. It is far more challenging to learn from someone you don't like (Consalvo & Maloch, 2015).

Returning to Dr. Botkin's engineering classes, he intentionally spotlights two students in each session. He wants to ensure that he is demonstrating that he values each of his learners and provides them his full attention, and that of the class, during the spotlight. As he says, "I am super careful about my body language all the time, but when I do a spotlight, I show the student that I am very interested. And really, I am. They know in advance but I don't tell the rest of the class. And they share interesting things. Then we do a question and answer period and it's great for building their efficacy and identity as engineers. But it started so that I could show students that I was interested in them as people."

REFLECTIVE WRITING

This is just for you. Who are the students at risk in your distance learning classroom? Use initials only. What barriers are you currently experiencing?

A "CHILLY" CLASSROOM

Some students keep us a bit more at arm's length. They may be reserved in nature, or distrustful of professors in general. Others exhibit problematic behaviors that disrupt the learning environment. In some cases, we just don't like a particular student, just rubbing you the wrong way and you're not even sure why. Unfortunately, the students we don't like, especially those we perceive as being low achieving, pay for it in terms of positive teacher attention. A study of differential teacher treatment of students (Good, 1987) found that low-achieving students

- Are criticized more often for failure
- Are praised less frequently
- Receive less feedback
- Are called on less often
- Have less eye contact from the teacher
- Have fewer friendly interactions with the teacher
- Experience acceptance of their ideas less often

Susan Almarode (University of Virginia, Nursing) explains how to convey warmth, trust, and empathy.

resources.corwin.com/ DLPlaybook-college

Each of these can just as easily occur in a distance classroom. There is another term for this: a *chilly classroom climate* in which some students do not feel they are valued and instead feel that "their presence . . . is at best peripheral, and at worst an unwelcome intrusion" (Hall & Sandler, 1982, p. 3). We do not in any way believe that our differential behaviors are conscious and intentional. One speculation is that because educators don't feel successful with students they view as lower achieving, we subconsciously avoid contact with them. After all, we were human beings long before we became educators, and as social animals we attempt to surround ourselves with people who make us feel good about ourselves. Students who are not making gains make us feel like failures, and so we detach ourselves even more.

Pamyla Yates (Blue Ridge Community College, English) explains how to convey warmth, trust, and empathy.

resources.corwin.com/ DLPlaybook-college

Now view Good's list from the opposite direction—students we see as being high achieving get more of us. Our attention, our contact, our interactions are more frequent, sustained, and growth producing. It is understandable that we gravitate to those students that make us feel successful as educators. But it is also a version of the Matthew effect, this time in attention rather than reading—the rich get richer while the poor get poorer (Stanovich, 1986). In this case, it's our positive attention that is gold.

REACHING THE HARD TO TEACH

In the College of Education at a major state university, faculty literally called every student in the majors housed in that department. They divided up the call list among departments and faculty, but every student got a phone call. Even the dean participated in this task. But they did not stop there. The dean's office maintained a running list of students that they were not able to reach or had not heard from during the semester. A concerted and targeted effort was made by the college to make contact with these students and ensure they were okay and to identify ways to better support them. Imagine flipping the switch on this narrative by intentionally increasing your positive attention efforts with students you have identified as being difficult to reach through distance learning.

We don't mean suddenly focusing all your attention on the three students that fall into that category while neglecting all the others. A quick pivot like that might be viewed as alarming or dismaying. However, waging a thoughtful campaign to change the dynamic is likely to have another benefit. Those students are likely to grow on you. We'll borrow advice attributed to Archbishop Desmond Tutu that sometimes you have to "act your way into being." In other words, sometimes the change in behavior precedes the change in perception.

Many of these behaviors seem to come naturally, at least when it comes to those students with whom we have a positive relationship. But it takes deliberate action to disrupt established communication patterns that are avoidant in nature. Identify the two or three students you want to target for increased positive attention. During live interactions, keep a tally for yourself about the following teacher-initiated behaviors.

SOMETIMES YOU HAVE TO "ACT YOUR WAY INTO BEING."

INTERACTION	STUDENT 1	STUDENT 2	STUDENT 3
Did I greet students by name when they entered the distance classroom?			
How many times did I use their names (not as a correction) during the session?			
Did I ask them a critical thinking question related to the content?			
Did I ask them a personal question?			
Did I pay them a compliment?			
How many times did I provide them with praise for learning performance?			

After you have collected data on yourself across several sessions, examine it and make some decisions about what you need to do more of and less of. In addition, reflect on any changes you have perceived in their reactions to you. It isn't always comfortable to look at these kinds of data, but it is something that courageous educators do because it fuels their own improvement. We'll harken back to the beginning of this module and the mindframes of great teachers: *I see assessment as informing my impact and next steps*.

REFLECTIVE WRITING

What am I noticing in the data I have collected? What changes have I noticed in these students?

Patterns and trends in the data	
Changes in identified students	
Actions and next steps	

INCREASE YOUR TOUCHPOINTS WITH ALL STUDENTS

Disney entertainment parks strive to provide every visitor with what they call a "world class experience." One focus of their efforts is the concept of touchpoints, which they define as ranging from personal interactions to the functional items such as the signage in their parking lots. There are parallels to the work that we do in distance learning environments. Our touchpoints include the interactions we have with students but also extend to the website we use on the learning management system, the email contact we have outside of class, and the directions we provide for asynchronous learning.

Given the increased challenge that distance learning poses, it is crucial that you develop tools and systems so that you can actively monitor the number and quality of touchpoint interactions with each student on your roster. Most distance learning schedules have far fewer hours of contact than in face-to-face instruction. Casual conversations in the hallway or the cafeteria aren't possible, and too often a misplaced focus on doing as much direct instruction as possible in live sessions has meant that interaction opportunities have decreased even more. Use these approaches to maximize ways to build and maintain relationships across the school year:

1. **Have a system for calling on students and noticing who hasn't participated**. Teachers call on students to respond to questions and to participate in learning tasks. However, the pattern of who is called upon is often uneven and may leave some students out of the discussion.

   An effective way to overcome the limitations of calling on students disproportionately is to use a method for randomly calling on students. This allows several goals to be achieved simultaneously. The most obvious is that it decreases the likelihood that some students will be overlooked. Many students have perfected the ability to remain unnoticed in distance classrooms, sitting quietly on the fringes of the discussion. While the goal of a random questioning method is not to put students on the spot, it is to encourage other voices in the classroom discourse. In addition, it gives the teacher a richer and more nuanced portrait of the level of understanding the class possesses at a moment in time. If the only students that are called on are the ones who know the answer (and are therefore more likely to volunteer), then the teacher is not aware of what may need to be retaught, and to whom. Don't use a random question method as a way to catch students off guard. Always announce that you are going to use a random question method. Pose the question and allow all students time to develop their response. Then, randomly call

IT ISN'T ALWAYS COMFORTABLE TO LOOK AT THESE KINDS OF DATA, BUT IT IS SOMETHING THAT COURAGEOUS EDUCATORS DO BECAUSE IT FUELS THEIR OWN IMPROVEMENT.

on a student. Ensure that you have students' attention before posing the question. This is respectful and contributes positively to the relationship between you and the student.

- **Use the site wheelofnames.com to create a spinner with all of your students names.** Then share your screen and see who is randomly selected.

- **Name cards on a ring.** Write names on index cards and punch a hole in the top left corner and place them in a 2-inch binder.

- **Pass it on.** After responding, allow the student to choose the next person. Be careful that this does not become a popularity contest.

- **Keep a tally on your class roster.** Simple tick marks let you know who has been talking and who hasn't.

ALWAYS ANNOUNCE THE STUDENT'S NAME AND MAKE SURE YOU HAVE THEIR ATTENTION BEFORE POSING THE QUESTION.

2. **Make sure every live session includes whole group and small group discussions.**

Without discussion opportunities, you have very few ways to use your students' names, ask nondirective and critical thinking questions, and demonstrate your unconditional regard for them. Use the "breakout room" feature to provide students opportunities to engage in dialogue with small groups of peers.

- **Curtail your lecture time** by recording asynchronous experiences and increase the opportunities for discussion when you are together.

- **Students can be assigned to develop questions** for use in discussions of readings that were completed asynchronously. The discussion director writes two or three discussion questions in advance of the session and shares them with the teacher. This achieves several goals, including expanding choice in learning and conveying your respect for them as scholars.

3. **If you assign discussion boards, actively participate in them.** Some distance learning classes use discussion boards for students to respond to a prompt and to one another. Few things are more discouraging, however, than wondering if the professor even reads them or just assigns a numerical score.

- Be an active presence on your discussion boards by replying regularly to student postings. You don't have to respond to all of them, but students should see your name regularly.

- Keep track of who you respond to so that you can be sure to distribute your attention equitably.

4. **Use "pop-up pedagogy" to increase touchpoints across the week.**
   Your live distance sessions are limited, but students should still be engaging with your content throughout the week. Increase the number of touchpoints outside of live distance sessions using an approach Fitzpatrick (2016) calls *pop-up pedagogy*. You know those ads that fly up onto your screen when you're looking at a website? Those are pop-ups. And while we don't mean that you literally are placing ads, think of pop-ups as ways for students to think about your class even when you're not in front of them. Here are some ideas:

   - Send messages to students several times a week.

     ○ A greeting with a motivational quote can be effective (e.g., "The expert in anything was once a beginner. Congratulations on improving your expertise in binomial equations!").

     ○ An intriguing question can be used to foreshadow upcoming content (e.g., "Have you wondered why your cell phone battery dies? We'll be discussing this in PHYS 101 on Monday. Bring your ideas!").

   - Post photos of student work on your learning management system. Ask students to submit pictures of them working with their peers online or of their work toward an assignment. For example, as students in art professor Nan Covert's photography class worked on their portfolios, she asked students to use visuals to document their progress. These images were shared with the class.

   - Craft an email newsletter or infograph each week explaining the previous week's learning and what they will be studying in the coming week. You don't need to make this fancy or extensive. These newsletters can also be posted on your website, but many students will miss this information unless they go to the website. Sending emails means that more students are likely to encounter the information.

   - Personalize directions for assignments by making a short video rather than only providing written directions. When you think about it, you rarely read written directions verbatim to a face-to-face class. Instead, you augment the written directions with your own verbal language. Let them see and hear you, not just read what you've written.

   - Use voice recording feedback tools on students' assignments. Not only is this faster than typing out written feedback, it's much easier to personalize it. Be sure to say the student's name, provide feedback about strengths and suggestions for next steps, and pose a thought-provoking question to keep the conversation going.

Of course, this is by no means an exhaustive list, and you probably have other ideas you are already using, or that you have heard colleagues discuss. Our intention is to spark your creative thinking for how to build and maintain faculty–student relationships during the semester or academic year.

NOTE TO SELF

How will you increase touchpoints for all your students?

How will you call on students?	
How will you notice who hasn't participated so you can re-engage them?	
What will you need to be mindful of to create more discussion opportunities during live distance sessions?	
How will you be a presence on your discussion boards?	
What is your "pop-up pedagogy" plan to stay connected with students when you are not in a live session?	

CONCLUSION

Quality faculty–student relationships are foundational to learning environments but can be more challenging in a distance learning one. Revisit the three to five quality indicators you recorded at the beginning of this module. Are there any you would change based on new learning? As a final task for this module, complete the following self-assessment so that you can identify where to target your efforts.

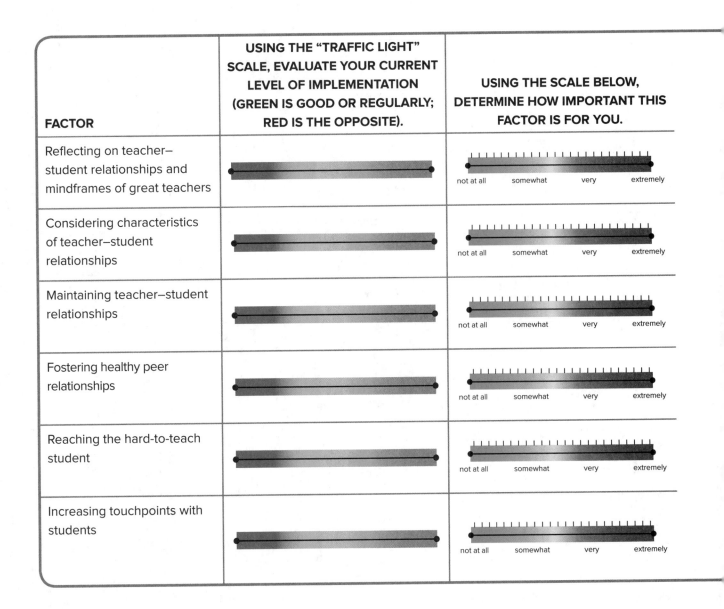

FACTOR	USING THE "TRAFFIC LIGHT" SCALE, EVALUATE YOUR CURRENT LEVEL OF IMPLEMENTATION (GREEN IS GOOD OR REGULARLY; RED IS THE OPPOSITE).	USING THE SCALE BELOW, DETERMINE HOW IMPORTANT THIS FACTOR IS FOR YOU.
Reflecting on teacher–student relationships and mindframes of great teachers		not at all somewhat very extremely
Considering characteristics of teacher–student relationships		not at all somewhat very extremely
Maintaining teacher–student relationships		not at all somewhat very extremely
Fostering healthy peer relationships		not at all somewhat very extremely
Reaching the hard-to-teach student		not at all somewhat very extremely
Increasing touchpoints with students		not at all somewhat very extremely

MODULE 4

TEACHER CREDIBILITY AT A DISTANCE

LEARNING INTENTIONS

- I am learning what is meant by teacher credibility.

- I am learning about different ways to maintain my credibility with students from a distance.

SUCCESS CRITERIA

- I can develop routines and procedures that ensure that trust is maintained in distance.

- I can demonstrate my competence using familiar routines and acknowledge new learning especially related to technology.

- I can bring passion to synchronous and asynchronous learning for my students.

- I can find ways to maintain immediacy with students in distance learning.

- I can support others in developing and maintaining their credibility.

Do your students believe that they can learn from you? If your answer is yes, they will likely learn a lot more. In fact, the effect size of teacher credibility, which is the label we give to the concept that students believe that they can learn from their teachers or professors, is 1.09. WOW! Right? It's powerful. But, like all of the influences that are likely to significantly accelerate learning, it's hard to accomplish. Importantly, the credibility teachers have with their students changes; it's dynamic. It's not the same for all students at the same time. In the last module, we talked about faculty–student relationships, which are important. Professors and students should have healthy, growth-producing relationships, in part because students learn more when these relationships are present. It's hard to imagine that a professor could be credible with students without a strong relationship. But our credibility extends to other areas, specifically trust, competence, dynamism or passion, and immediacy or perceived closeness.

Before we ask you to draw on your expertise, let's visit a distance class meeting and see what we notice about credibility. The students in religion professor Mary Kyger's contemporary theologies course had been learning about the conflict between history and faith in contemporary theological movements in South America. Two days before the test, Dr. Kyger provided her students with a practice version of the exam. They could take this practice version as many times as they wanted but they had to identify areas in which they needed more practice or additional learning. As Dr. Kyger said on the video that introduced the practice test, "You have worked hard with me on this topic and I hope you'll trust me and yourselves to complete the practice versions on your own. That way, you'll know what you know and where you still need learning. I'll be online for three hours and you can pop in and share your screen any time that you want. We can work together on any of the practice items that give you trouble. I know you know this material. I'm not here to trick you. Your assessment will look a lot similar to the practice version. The assessment will focus on the essential themes and understandings."

When the students clicked on the icon to take the test, the first thing that popped up was a hint, which read "Remember, we need to identify the essential characteristics of theological movements. Oh, but you already knew that." The students were presented with a question that was related to what defines a theological movement. Dr. Kyger had posed a question that required them to synthesize information rather than simply regurgitate facts. This is what they were accustomed to and had come to expect in class discussions, assignments, and exams.

One of her students quickly messaged Dr. Kyger to ask, "Do we have to evaluate which characteristic is the most significant one in describing theological movements?" Almost instantly, Dr. Kyger responded, "Nope, as long as you support your response with evidence, I am most interested in how you are making meaning of this content. Message me if you want to talk further. Or share your list of characteristics with me so we can chat."

The student replied, "Thanks. Actually, I just wanted to see if you would really respond."

It may be easier to see a professor's credibility in a physical classroom, but we hope you noticed several things about this small slice of Dr. Kyger's teaching. She is trustworthy. Her students know what to expect from her and she does not try to trick them. She seems competent, but we would probably know more about her students' perceptions of her competence if we could see one of her classes in which she demonstrates her thinking or coaches their learning. In terms of passion, the video seemed as if she were coming through the screen. She was dressed for success, animated, and excited. And finally, even though they were apart, students knew that they could reach her and that she was there.

IMPORTANTLY, THE CREDIBILITY TEACHERS HAVE WITH THEIR STUDENTS CHANGES; IT'S DYNAMIC. IT'S NOT THE SAME FOR ALL STUDENTS AT THE SAME TIME.

DRAWING ON MY EXPERTISE

Consider the following questions about your past experiences with credibility.

1. How have I established trust with my students?

2. How do I demonstrate competence to my students?

3. How do I display my dynamism to my students?

4. How do I ensure that my students feel close to me?

Let's explore teacher credibility further and then identify ways to develop and maintain your credibility from a distance.

Dominique Smith (Cuyamaca Community College, Social Work) discusses teacher credibility in higher education.

resources.corwin.com/ DLPlaybook-college

TEACHER CREDIBILITY DEFINED

At the basic level, faculty need to be seen as believable, convincing, and capable of persuading students that they can be successful. Students know which professors can make a difference. If you don't believe us, visit any online professor rating website. As we have previously noted, "The dynamic of teacher credibility is *always* at play" (Fisher, Frey, & Hattie, 2016, p. 10). Thankfully, there are specific actions that any teacher can take to increase credibility in each of the following four areas (Fisher, Frey, & Smith, 2020). This includes faculty at colleges and universities.

TRUST

Students need to know that their professors really care about them as individuals and have their best academic and social interests at heart. Students also want to know that their professors are true to their word and are reliable. Here are a few points about trust:

1. If you make a promise, work to keep it (or explain why you could not).

2. Tell students the truth about their performance (they know when their work is below standard and wonder why you are telling them otherwise).

3. Don't spend all of your time trying to catch students in the wrong (and yet be honest about the impact that their choices have on their peers and their professional career).

4. Examine any negative feelings you have about specific students (they sense it and it compromises the trust within the virtual classroom).

IT MAY SEEM SIMPLE, BUT WE HAVE WITNESSED A DECREASE IN THE TRUST STUDENTS HAVE IN THEIR TEACHERS WHEN THEY SEE THEIR TEACHERS AS UNRELIABLE.

As Covey (2008) noted in *The Speed of Trust*, when it exists, things go faster. These more generic recommendations will continue to serve us well in a distance learning format. But there are additional considerations. In fact, Hoy and Tschannen-Moran (2003) identified five elements for trust to be developed and maintained:

- **Benevolence:** Confidence that one's well-being or something one cares about will be protected by the trusted party . . . the assurance that others will not exploit one's vulnerability or take advantage even when the opportunity is available.

- **Honesty:** The trusted person's character, integrity, and authenticity . . . acceptance of responsibility for one's actions and not distorting the truth in order to shift blame to another.

- **Openness:** The extent to which relevant information is shared . . . openness signals reciprocal trust.

- **Reliability:** Consistency of behavior and knowing what to expect from others . . . a sense of confidence that one's needs will be met in positive ways.

- **Competency:** The ability to perform as expected and according to standards appropriate to the task at hand. (von Frank, 2010, p. 2)

As kinesiology professor Chris Blankenship noted, "Students ask me questions and expect an honest answer. It's the same whether we are face-to-face or online. But I noticed that when they are at home, sometimes they ask me questions that wouldn't really be asked in a traditional classroom. I need to answer, but also remember that I'm still their professor."

We have found that teachers are being asked a number of questions that have them searching for appropriate answers. The lack of physical proximity and the fact that they are home seems to invite questions that might not have been asked in the classrooms, hallways, or offices of academic buildings. Our advice is that you answer honestly when you can and that you are clear about the reasons when there are questions you cannot answer. For example, Dr. Blankenship shared a story about how his KIN 300 students peppered him with questions about why university leadership was not responding more to the virus and then began to list things they felt needed to be done. Immediately another student asked if Dr. Blankenship believed that the pandemic was real. Although engaging in a discussion that disparages senior leadership, it is important to share with students the actions of the university to respond to the current crisis—value free. Furthermore, providing students with options for seeking more information and support keeps the focus on supporting our students. And you know where this will likely go. Dr. Blankenship reported that he was asked who he would vote for in the upcoming presidential election. As I told them, "We have private places to vote in the US called polls so that people can vote what is in their heart and without judgement."

It may seem simple, but we have witnessed a decrease in the trust students have in their professors when they see their professors as unreliable. And it's as simple as being late for an online learning session. As one student relayed, "She never logs in on time and always looks like she rushed to get logged in. She's late a lot. And she gets frustrated when the technology does not work well and often ends class before we're supposed to be finished. She has basically written off the semester."

Another student relayed her concerns about her curriculum and instruction course in education. The actions of her professor compromised her trust and thus lessened the credibility of that professor. In this specific situation, it was based on the feedback that was promised but never received. The student shared that, "On the posts we are required to share on the class discussion boards, everybody gets a 10. It doesn't matter if we provide in-depth comments and reflections about issues in curriculum development and implementation. Sometimes we simply agree with another post. We just all get 10. It's like she doesn't care. And we are

Susan Almarode (University of Virginia, Nursing) shares her story about developing her passion for nursing to enhance credibility.

resources.corwin.com/DLPlaybook-college

given online reading quizzes that are automatically graded by the computer or a graduate assistant. We are all sure that she does not even know our scores. And when we submit assignments, the comments are just like 'good work' or 'I see your point' or 'that's interesting.' It doesn't help you get any better." Lack of honest feedback broke the trust she had with the teacher.

On a more positive note, another student reported that his architectural design professor records audio files and talks about each student's work. As this student shared, "We get a personal commentary back on our work. He talks directly to us, each person, and tells us what he is thinking when he looks at what we did. He talks about things that are effective and things that need revising or where we made mistakes. And he tells us what the next step is. I like it when he says, like, 'your inclusion of many sources of natural lighting is a great way to brighten up the space. But I think it might be a little too much given the access points to the bedroom. I think you might want to be more subtle in the lighting design. Plus, you allow for a greater palette of colors with this more subtle approach. Do you want to talk further about the art of being subtle?' That really got me and so I scheduled a time to talk with him to learn more. I know he's gonna be honest and that it will make me better."

NOTE TO SELF

Based on the descriptions of trust, what ideas do you have for maintaining and enhancing this aspect of credibility at a distance?

_____

_____

_____

_____

_____

_____

_____

_____

_____

_____

_____

COMPETENCE

In addition to trust, students want to know that their professors are active in their respective fields, know their stuff, and know how to engage with learners that are not yet experts. They expect an appropriate level of expertise and accuracy from their professors. Further, students measure competence by the ability of the professor to deliver instruction that is coherent and organized. They expect learning experiences that are well paced and the information is accurate.

1. Make sure you know the content well and be honest when a question arises that you are not sure about (this requires planning in advance).

2. Organize lesson delivery in a cohesive and coherent way.

3. Consider your nonverbal behaviors that communicate competence, such as the position of your hands when you talk with students or the facial expressions you make (students notice defensive positions and nonverbal indications that they are not valued when they speak).

We have several modules later in this playbook devoted to developing and enhancing our collective competence in distance learning. If distance learning is new for you, you'll probably feel like a beginning teacher again. You can choose to think of this as a wonderful learning opportunity or a royal pain. The task is the same, but how you view it can influence your efforts, the stress you experience, and the satisfaction you receive.

As we discuss further in Module 6, Engaging Tasks at a Distance, it's impossible to keep up with all the distance learning tools available. We have found solace in knowing that the functions have remained essentially the same, even though the tools change regularly. Consider the need to search for information. Some of us remember traveling to the library and looking up information in the card catalog and then going to find the book on a shelf someplace. We have not stopped searching for information, but the tools we use to find that information have changed (and they'll continue to change throughout our lifetimes). We cannot be competent, or even knowledgeable, about every tool out there. But we can learn some new tools that serve the functions we need to accomplish.

When music professor Shirley Masters first engaged in teaching MUS 141: Music Theory I from a distance, she was nervous. She was worried that she would "do it wrong" and "make a fool of herself" in front of her students. Her first live class meeting via computer video was not great but she told her students that she was learning and how excited she was. As she said, "So, this is my first time doing this. I am a little nervous but I'm also excited. At the end, I want to ask for feedback. I want to be sure that you're learning and I'm willing to make adjustments so that you can learn from me and each other." At the end of her first class meeting, when she invited students to provide feedback, they were uniformly kind and offered a number of ideas for her to consider. For example, one student suggested that she use the reaction buttons. Another student hoped that she would annotate on the screen so that they could track where she was. And a third student requested that they get to keep the same

THE TASK IS THE SAME, BUT HOW YOU VIEW IT CAN INFLUENCE YOUR EFFORTS, THE STRESS YOU EXPERIENCE, AND THE SATISFACTION YOU RECEIVE.

breakout groups during the session so that they could keep adding to their discussions. Relieved that it went well, Dr. Masters called her department chair and excitedly reported, "I think that they actually learned something from me today. And I learned more about what they want from me. It feels really good and their ideas are great. I'm going to contact the technology office right now so that I can practice these ideas before class next week."

Interestingly, when professors change their instructional strategies too frequently, students believe that they are not competent. As one student said, "I'm not sure she knows what she is doing because she tries something different every time." To build on our competency, learning routines should be predictable and understandable to students. That's not to say that change is forbidden, but rather that you plan some tasks that students come to expect. Some variety is good, but so is consistency.

Danielle Brown, a chemistry professor, has found the ideal balance between mixing things up and establishing a flow in her classes. She sums it up this way:

> I flow each week so that students know what to expect. Generally, the same flow each week. Of course, the content changes and I might add a few tasks here and there, but my students know what to expect from this class. For example, they know on Mondays they're going to see me on video. I've recorded a lot of information in short bits for them and I've embedded quizzes into the videos. They can do these over and over to get them all right. There's no penalty for practice. On Wednesdays, they know that we're going to have a reading. I read live with them, modeling my thinking and asking questions in the chat to build conceptual understanding around ideas like catalysts, kinetics, etc. . . . I offer this several times each Wednesday and they can attend any session that they want. I know that sounds strange to some people, but my students like choices as they balance their own "work from home environments." On Wednesday, they also know that they will have many opportunities to relate the concept to authentic applications outside of class. Assignments on Wednesday require them to find current information that relates to the topic we're studying that week. They have until Friday to submit their conceptually based assignments that requires them to integrate some of the background knowledge we built on Monday. On Fridays, they have collaborative tasks and virtual labs. These change, but they know that collaboration and experiments are Friday. I also offer tutorials several times per day on Thursday. I require some students to attend and make them optional for others. If the initial assessment information tells me that a student needs more time and attention in a particular area (e.g., stoichiometry, oxidation-reduction reactions), I schedule them for sessions. In addition, I schedule all of the students with plans from the Office for Disability Services (ODS) in these sessions for the added time. On Fridays, we also have quizzes and writing tasks. They can take the quizzes over as many times as they want, provided that they explain why an answer was incorrect. When they do, I clear the attempt and they take it again. I think that this predictability really helps them navigate the content. In fact, I think they pay more attention to the content because they know what is expected of them.

SOME VARIETY IS GOOD, BUT SO IS CONSISTENCY.

James Wangberg (University of Wyoming at Laramie, Entomology) describes how to leverage and maintain competence.

resources.corwin.com/ DLPlaybook-college

Based on the descriptions of competence, what ideas do you have for maintaining and enhancing this aspect of credibility at a distance?

DYNAMISM

This dimension of teacher credibility focuses on the passion professors bring to the classroom and their content. It is really about your ability to communicate enthusiasm for your subject and your students. And it's about developing spirited lessons that capture students' interest. To improve dynamism,

Shayna North (Cuyamaca Community College, Nutrition) explains how to let our passion shine from a distance.

resources.corwin.com/ DLPlaybook-college

YOUR PASSION DID NOT CHANGE BECAUSE YOU ARE TEACHING FROM A DISTANCE. MAKE SURE THAT YOUR STUDENTS KNOW THAT.

1. **Rekindle your passion for the content you teach** by focusing on the aspects that got you excited as a student—undergraduate or graduate. Remember why you wanted to be a scholar in this field or discipline and teach the content you wanted to introduce to your students. Students notice when their professors are bored by the content and when their professors aren't really interested in the topic. We think that a professor's motto should be "Make content interesting!"

2. **Consider the relevance of your lessons.** Does the content lend itself to application outside the class? Do students have opportunities to learn about themselves and their critical thinking skills? Does the content help them become civic minded and engaged in the community? Does it connect to universal human experiences or ask students to grapple with ethical concerns? When there isn't relevance, students check out and may be compliant learners rather than committed learners.

3. **Seek feedback from trusted colleagues about your lesson delivery.** Ask colleagues to sit in on a distance lesson to focus on the energy you bring and the impact on students' demeanors, rather than the individual instructional strategies you use. Students respond to the passion and energy in a lesson, even if they didn't initially think they would be interested.

Wangberg (1996), an entomology professor, argues that there are at least four ways to demonstrate passion in the classroom. He notes that "the best teachers are people who are passionate about their subject *and* passionate about sharing that subject with others" (p. 199). Wangberg created a passion inventory (Figure 4.1). We found this tool to be useful as a reflection guide. It will help you assess your current level of dynamism and might point to some things that you can do to increase your score, and then perhaps your students' learning. Take the passion inventory. What surprises you about the results? Where do you see areas for growth? Who will you need to enlist to support your growth?

Your passion did not change because you are teaching from a distance. Make sure that your students know that. We're almost embarrassed to say this, but your dynamism shows in what you wear to class. Consider this: If you wouldn't wear it to the building, don't wear it on camera with your students. Students expect their professors to look a certain way. We are not suggesting that you must wear a tie or business clothes. We are saying that how you look matters and failure to consider this can compromise your credibility. As one student said, "I think she forgot we had class. She looked like she just got out of bed and didn't even comb her hair." That's not good.

Figure 4.1 Passion Inventory

Score 1 point for each item that depicts you or your students.

1. I am enthusiastic about my teaching. It is something I enjoy and look forward to doing. It is a fun, exciting, and stimulating activity for me.

2. My students can sense my enthusiasm. They have conveyed this impression to me in their evaluations or in their personal comments.

3. I am continuing to learn. I am active in research. I read and attempt to keep up with the appropriate literature. I obtain new information from my students.

4. My students are witnesses to my interest in learning. They see me doing research, reading the literature, conversing with colleagues, participating in professional conferences, and actively engaging with my discipline.

5. I can get absorbed in my work, but not so self-absorbed that others are excluded. I am likely to share what interests me and bring my interests to the attention of others.

6. I continue to try new approaches in my teaching. The class that I have taught several times is different and better than when I began. Sometimes I try things that do not work, but these failures do not prevent me from taking new risks or experimenting with my teaching.

7. I care about my students. I want them to learn, to realize their potential, and to succeed in class and in other useful and challenging endeavors.

Your Score:

    7 pts.   Powerfully passionate!

    6 pts.   Pridefully passionate

    5 pts.   Pretty passionate

    <5 pts.   Seek help from a passion professional!

Source: Wangberg, J. K. (1996). Teaching with a passion. *American Entomologist, 42,* 199–200. Oxford: Oxford University Press. Used with permission.

But dynamism is more than an outward appearance. It's also about the excitement you bring to the sessions, both synchronous and asynchronous. There are a number of ways to demonstrate enthusiasm, including the tone in your voice, the emotional stories you tell, or the presentation techniques you use. Regardless of the approach, students should know that you care about the content.

Students judge our dynamism based on the instructional materials that we use. Old, wordy slides are deadly. Extra slides cost nothing so please do not crowd all of the information on a single slide. Space it out. Use visuals. Change fonts and text size. Add multimedia when it is useful. Mix it up a bit and show students that you cared enough to prepare something that was interesting.

A freshman shared his thinking about two professors and how their use of visuals changed his perceptions of each class.

> In my History of Latin America class, the professor reads from a slide with like 800 words. Well, not really, but it seems like it. The words are small

and we try to copy things down when she's talking. It's crazy. You can't even really listen to the video because you're trying to write. But in my oceanography class, the professor uses a lot more slides. Like there is one idea on each one and there is a picture that helps us understand what she's saying. I feel like I'm really learning about the world's oceans, and I didn't even like science before. This is a general education requirement for me. But I'm getting it because the information is clear and there are lots of examples. It's like she took the time to really plan it out for us and then put together information to help us understand it. In my Latin America class, it's just like a rush of info and we aren't even sure what is important. I check out a lot, really, because I get bored and frustrated.

NOTE TO SELF

Based on the descriptions of dynamism, what ideas do you have for maintaining and enhancing this aspect of credibility at a distance?

IMMEDIACY

This final construct of teacher credibility focuses on accessibility and relatability as perceived by students. The concept of immediacy was introduced by social psychologist Albert Mehrabian (1971) who noted that "people are drawn toward persons and things they like, evaluate highly, and prefer; and they avoid or move away from things they dislike, evaluate negatively, or do not prefer" (p. 1). Professors who move around the room and are easy to interact with increase students' perception of immediacy. That's hard to do in a distance space. But have you considered visiting their breakout rooms? Have you considered using student names during your live sessions and making sure every student hears their name every day? Professors need to be accessible and yet there needs to be a sense of urgency that signals to students that their learning is important to you.

1. Get to know something personal about each student, as students know when you don't know their names or anything about them.

2. Teach with urgency but not to the point that it causes undo stress for them. That said, students want to know that their learning matters and that you are not wasting their time.

3. Start the class on time and use every minute wisely. This means that there are tasks students can complete while you engage in routine tasks such as taking attendance and that you have a series of sponge activities ready when lessons run short. Students notice when time is wasted. And when there is "free time," they believe that their learning is not an urgent consideration of their teachers.

Consider the following examples of general things you can do to ensure that your students feel close to you irrespective of the format of the class:

- Gesture when talking

- Look at students and smile while talking

- Call students by name

- Use *we* and *us* to refer to the class

- Invite students to provide feedback

- Use vocal variety (pauses, inflections, stress, emphasis) when talking to the class

Marcy Cervantes, Spanish language professor, uses current events when engaging in conversational Spanish with her students during SPAN 335: Spanish Literature. She finds that this improves her immediacy because her students see her interacting with topics and events that are relevant to their lives and connected to what they are reading. Dr. Cervantes has conversations throughout the class meeting, weaving in the text they are working with and current events when they naturally fit into the learning focus. "Each time I start a conversation about a current event related to a text we are working with, I invite students to share their thinking and perspective. Students have to talk about the text, make connections to current events, and then support their thinking with evidence. If we are reading a novel that brings to life the struggles of Spanish immigrants, I engage my students in conversations around how we see that playing out today in the United States."

Dr. Cervantes asks her students questions to gain a better understanding of their perspective and how their generation is making sense of the world around them. She always invites students to share their own story. She then ties this into the characters in the fictional text and follows up with more questions. "I often invite students to agree or disagree and then justify their response. And then a third student was invited to say how they knew this." This helps Dr. Cervantes maintain her immediacy with her students, at a distance.

Geology professor Brenda Davis is widely known as a faculty member who supports students' learning in all of her classes. In addition, she meets with small groups of students for additional support each day. As she says, "I keep my groups to five so that I can maintain a sense of community with them. I usually do some preteaching so that they have background information before they are in class. I also work on study strategies with them. It keeps us connected. I keep my camera on so that students can see me. And I make sure that I'm looking at them, even when their cameras are off. It's hard, but I think it's really important for them to feel connected to me."

CONCLUSION

When a professor is *not* perceived as credible, students tune out. They fail to log in, they fail to complete tasks, they fail to engage with peers; they fail. And quite frankly, we can't afford for students to do so. We need students to engage, to trust their professors, and to choose to participate in their learning. The four aspects of teacher credibility—trust, competence, dynamism, and immediacy—can help do just that. As a final task for this module, now that you have a sense of the value of teacher credibility, complete the following self-assessment.

FACTOR	USING THE "TRAFFIC LIGHT" SCALE, EVALUATE YOUR CURRENT LEVEL OF IMPLEMENTATION (GREEN IS GOOD OR REGULARLY; RED IS THE OPPOSITE).	USING THE SCALE BELOW, DETERMINE HOW IMPORTANT THIS FACTOR IS FOR YOU.
Trust		not at all somewhat very extremely
Competence		not at all somewhat very extremely
Dynamism		not at all somewhat very extremely
Immediacy		not at all somewhat very extremely

MODULE 5

TEACHER CLARITY AT A DISTANCE

LEARNING INTENTIONS

- I am learning how to increase clarity in distance learning.
- I am learning about learning intentions and success criteria.

SUCCESS CRITERIA

- I can describe various aspects of teacher clarity.
- I can use the three clarity questions to plan distance learning experiences.
- I can analyze standards to identify concepts and skills.
- I can develop learning intentions that ensure students know what they are supposed to learn.
- I can develop success criteria that provide students ideas about what learning looks like.
- I can discuss the relevance of the learning expectations with students.

Big Ideas

Do your students know what they are supposed to be learning? Or do they see the class as a list of things to do? There is a big difference between these two. When students know what they are expected to learn, they are more likely to learn it. At some point in every class meeting, students should know what they are supposed to learn. Before we go much further into this topic, it's important to note the first part of the last sentence. We did not say at the outset of the lessons they should know what they are learning. At some point, they should. There are a number of valid reasons for withholding the purpose, or learning intention, until later. For example, the students in Allison Beaty's accounting course (ACTG 475) are being introduced to the techniques for gathering, summarizing, and analyzing information from financial statements. At the beginning of the class meeting, students were put into breakout rooms and provided three different sets of financial statements. Using guiding questions shared with learners in the chat box, the small groups were asked to compare and contrast the three sets of financial statements. They were asked to record their observations, questions, and inferences in their notes. After selecting a spokesperson, the small groups returned to the main room. In their live session, Dr. Beaty guided them through a discussion about what they observed, questioned, and inferred from the statements, creating a graphic organizer to record the students' thinking. Then, she let them know the purpose of this class meeting, which was to understand the process by which forensic accountants approach tax returns. The topics included an introduction to the techniques for gathering, summarizing, and analyzing information from financial statements. The learning intentions did not focus on tax returns, per se, but rather on looking at them with a critical eye. Dr. Beaty wanted to activate

Jamie Frueh (Bridgewater College, Political Science) discusses teacher clarity in higher education.

resources.corwin.com/ DLPlaybook-college

her students' background knowledge before focusing on the expected learning.

There is more to teacher clarity than learning intentions. Fendick (1990) describes four practices that combine to create clarity:

1. **Clarity of organization**: Tasks, assignments, and activities include links to the objectives and outcomes of learning (what we call learning intentions and success criteria).

2. **Clarity of explanation**: Information is relevant, accurate, and comprehensible to students.

3. **Clarity of examples and guided practice**: The lesson includes information that is illustrative and illuminating as students gradually move to independence, making progress with less support from the teacher.

4. **Clarity of assessment of student learning**: The teacher is regularly seeking out and acting upon the feedback they receive from students, especially through their verbal and written responses.

Teacher clarity has a respectable effect size of 0.75. In other words, it's a potential accelerator of students' learning. As we noted with other topics in this book, there are not studies of teacher clarity in distance learning. Instead, we are taking what we know from the classroom and applying it to other environments. Having said that, it's hard to imagine that simply completing a bunch of random tasks will cause learning. If our classes are reduced to a checklist of things to do, students may complete those tasks without developing a deep understanding of their own learning and the purpose or relevance of that learning.

This module focuses on some of the aspects of teacher clarity described by Fendick. Future modules will focus on other aspects, such as examples and guided practice, assessment, and lesson tasks. In this module, our attention centers on helping students understand **what they are supposed to learn, why that is important, and how they will know if they learned it**. We have organized this into three questions that contribute to teacher clarity (Fisher, Frey, & Hattie, 2016):

- What am I learning today?

- Why am I learning it?

- How will I know that I learned it?

DRAWING ON MY EXPERTISE

Consider the following questions about your past experiences with teacher clarity.

1. How have I established learning expectations for students?

2. How do I ensure students know what success looks like?

3. How do I align tasks with learning expectations?

4. How do I design assessments of learning expectations?

START WITH THE STANDARDS AND COMPETENCIES

Accreditation standards and professional competencies represent what each student is expected to know, understand, and be able to do within individual classes and across programs of study. They guide the instructional decision-making for professors who work in the program. In our colleges and universities, these standards and competencies are on file and have been approved by Academic Affairs, the State Council for Higher Education, and the accrediting body of the college or university. These are not just documents that we are obligated to submit to our department chairs, deans, or Provost. Instead, these documents lay the foundation for what students are learning, why they are learning it, and how they and we know they are successful. Often, professors use instructional materials that are aligned with those standards and competencies (well, they are supposed to, anyway). These materials include textbooks, supplemental materials, and online resources. For example, how do you decide which textbook or course pack to use in your abnormal psychology, chemistry, set theory, or alternative fuels class? In some cases, the authors of the instructional materials have analyzed the standards and created textbooks, course packs, and supplemental resources that align to those standards and competencies. Sometimes they're good, and other times they're not so good. And sometimes professors reorganize the materials to create a pathway for learning for their students. To our thinking, professors have to know the standards and competencies for both the program and their courses if they are going to make informed decisions about learning expectations and assessments.

WHAT AM I LEARNING TODAY?

WHY AM I LEARNING IT?

HOW WILL I KNOW THAT I LEARNED IT?

There are a number of ways to analyze expectations. A simple way is to take a look at the nouns (or noun phrases) and verbs (or verb phrases) in the standards or competencies. This provides clarity about the concepts (nouns) and skills (verbs) that students must master. This analysis can also help professors understand the type of thinking required or the depth of knowledge needed to be successful. For example, some standards focus on one idea, while others focus on several ideas. And still others focus on how ideas relate to one another or how ideas can be extended.

Let's look at a few examples. To do this on your own, we suggest asking your department head or program coordinator for the curriculum documents associated with your course or courses. The standards and competencies are listed in that document.

Steve Ralston, a biology professor, is looking at the expectations submitted to the university's accrediting body and the State Council for High Education to ensure he and his students are clear about what they are to learning in BIO 101 and what success looks like for his students.

SCOPE OF COURSE

Basic principles of general biology as they relate to the cellular, organismic, and population levels of organization. Includes cell ultrastructure and function, energy transfer, reproduction, genetics, evolution, diversity of organisms, and ecology.

SPECIFIC COURSE OBJECTIVES

The successful student will:

1. demonstrate proper safety in the laboratory;
2. use metric units and readily convert between units;
3. properly use and maintain the compound microscope;
4. describe the difference between science and non-science;
5. discuss the characteristics of experimentation and observation;
6. design simple experiments;
7. describe the structure of an atom;
8. describe chemical bonds (covalent and ionic);
9. discuss the pH scale and the characteristics of acids and bases;
10. compare proteins, lipids, carbohydrates and nucleic acids;
11. compare procaryotic and eucaryotic cells;
12. discuss transport of materials across biological membranes;
13. discuss the Laws of Thermodynamics;
14. compare mitosis and meiosis;
15. predict patterns of inheritance based on Mendel's Laws;
16. discuss human genetic disorders;
17. compare DNA and RNA;
18. describe the process of protein synthesis;
19. compare gene regulation in eucaryotic and procaryotic cells;
20. compare aerobic cellular respiration and photosynthesis;
21. discuss mechanisms of evolution;
22. compare the five kingdoms in the Whittaker Classification System;
23. compare phylogenetic trends in the plant kingdom;
24. compare phylogenetic trends in the animal kingdom;
25. describe energy flow and nutrient cycling in ecosystems;
26. describe ecological succession;
27. compare aquatic and terrestrial ecosystems;
28. compare exponential and logistic growth;
29. discuss the impact of humans on ecosystems.

Dr. Ralston noted that the concepts (nouns) students need to learn included

- Cellular, organismic, and population levels of organization
- Cell ultrastructure and function
- Energy transfer
- Reproduction
- Genetics
- Evolution
- Diversity of organisms
- Ecology

And the skills (verbs) students need to learn included

- Demonstrate
- Use
- Describe
- Discuss
- Compare
- Contrast

AT SOME POINT IN EVERY CLASS MEETING, STUDENTS SHOULD KNOW WHAT THEY ARE SUPPOSED TO LEARN.

For Dr. Ralston, this analysis of the standards and competencies will help him focus on what really matters for this particular course. Notice the skills are all related to higher-order thinking and do not include skills like name, identify, recognize. This will be very helpful for both Dr. Ralston and his students. We will come back to this idea in the next module.

Some courses within programs of study are not as interconnected as Dr. Ralston's BIO 101 course. For example, a general education world history course may have a specific standard that reads

> *Explain how the ideology of the French Revolution led France to develop from constitutional monarchy to democratic despotism to the Napoleonic empire.*

The concepts include

- Ideology
- French Revolution
- Constitutional monarchy
- Democratic despotism
- Napoleonic empire

Again, there is only one skill:

- Explain

Are you noticing a trend? There are often many concepts in a standard and only a few skills (and sometimes only one). But the skills are illusive. What does it mean, for example, to *explain* in the context of that history standard? Can you accomplish that skill orally, or does it need to be written? What makes for a good explanation? These are the questions that plague professors and are worthy of much discussion. If the standards are assessed on a summative examination, that can provide some clues about the ways in which accrediting bodies and professional organizations view the skills. But that is not always the case, and lack of understanding about the ways in which skills are taught and assessed can lead to further equity gaps or devoting time to what is "neat" to know and not what students "need" to know.

NOTE TO SELF

Let's practice. Identify a standard or competency that you will teach. Analyze the statement or statements for the required concepts and skills.

Standard(s)/Competencies

Concepts (nouns)

Skills (verbs)

CREATE A FLOW OF LEARNING: PLANNING FOR CLASS

When the standards or competencies to be taught and mastered have been analyzed, it's time to create a flow of learning. Which skills or concepts come first? What comes later? In some places, this is called a *learning progression*. There is not one right way to flow lessons, but there are probably wrong ways. Some ideas build on other ideas. Some skills are prerequisites to others. But sometimes the order doesn't really matter and it's more of a personal preference.

Daniel Haverlack, an education professor, uses a planning template to create the flow of learning for his elementary science methods course (see Figure 5.1). A blank version of the planning template can be found in the appendix. It can also be downloaded from this book's companion website (resources.corwin.com/ DLPlaybook-college) for ease of use. Notice that the template is organized for a week, not individual class meetings. We will get to daily learning intentions later. Also notice that the planning template includes activities and assessment opportunities as well as instructional materials. Before putting content online, teachers or teams of teachers can pace out the flow of learning to ensure that students have opportunities to master the standards and competencies. Further, this template includes a place to address the vocabulary demands of the learning. Teaching vocabulary well is important as words serve as labels for concepts. Understanding a text is significantly influenced by vocabulary knowledge. Writing well is also influenced by vocabulary knowledge. That's probably why the effect size of vocabulary at 0.63 is so strong.

In addition, the template provides an opportunity to describe supports for students with disabilities or those that are at risk due to their own circumstances with distance learning. Professors can plan additional supports for other students as well, but our experience with distance learning suggests that teachers must pay special attention to the learning needs of students with disabilities. When teachers plan for these needs in advance, rather than reacting to them later, students are likely to learn more. It's a key principal of Universal Design for Learning (CAST, 2018).

Figure 5.1 Sample Planning Template for Elementary Science Methods, Week 1

Standards/ Competencies	Topic (Learning Progressions)	Week	In-Class Activities	Formative Assessment Extend—Review— Assess—Reteach	Texts and Resources
1. Methods. a. Understanding of the needed knowledge, skills, dispositions, and processes to support learners in achievement of the standards of learning in science for all grade levels b. Understanding of current research on the brain, its role in learning, and implications for instruction	Qualities of effective elementary science teachers; what does it mean to be a good learner in science?	1	Oil, Food Coloring, and Large Plastic Test Tubes Laboratory; Text rendering task with article on "good learners" in science; Think-pair-share with definition of science and why science should be taught in the elementary school classroom	See—Think—Wonder Brainstorming Task; Think—Puzzle—Explore Graphic Organizer; Think-Pair-Share; Exit Ticket	Good Learner article; Laboratory supplies; Google Slides; Mentimeter poll

Summative Assessment Competency

- Lesson Plan (provide lesson planning rubric, student work analysis, and lesson plan reflection rubric)

Content and Academic Vocabulary

Objectives

Unpacking Standards

Curriculum Framework

Standards of Learning

Testing Blueprint

Learning Progressions

Dispositions

Accommodations and Modifications for Students With Disabilities

Cloze style foldables and notes

Examples of lesson plans

Lesson plan templates

CLARITY

NOTE TO SELF

Let's practice. Based on the standard(s)/competencies you analyzed, what might be a reasonable order to teach the concepts and skills?

Concepts (nouns)	Skills (verbs)

Flow of Concepts and Skills

1. _____

2. _____

3. _____

4. _____

5. _____

6. _____

7. _____

8. _____

CREATE LEARNING INTENTIONS

As part of each lesson, students should know what they are expected to learn. These are the learning intentions, which others call *objectives*, *learning targets*, or *learning goals*. There are differences for each of these terms, but we are not interested in the semantics. Rather, we care that students know what they are supposed to be learning. This is especially important in distance learning as students tell us that they get lost in the tasks and are sometimes not sure what they are supposed to be learning. As Katy Brittingham, an elementary education student, noted, "The professors always let us know what we're learning. And not just one time. Like many times, they remind us. And we talk about what we learned and what we still need to learn. When I'm online, there aren't as many reminders. And I try to get the work done but sometimes I don't know what I was supposed to be learning and then I don't do so well on the assessment."

WE CARE THAT STUDENTS KNOW WHAT THEY ARE SUPPOSED TO BE LEARNING. THIS IS ESPECIALLY IMPORTANT IN DISTANCE LEARNING.

As an example of learning intentions, physics professor Thomas Klein identified three major areas of learning based on his analysis of the competencies for his conceptual physics course:

> *Energy is required to separate positive and negative charge carriers; charge separation produces an electrical potential difference that can be used to drive current in circuits.*

Dr. Klein decided that the flow of learning would be

- Current, potential difference, and energy flow (4 hours)
- Resistance (4 hours)
- Circuit analysis and design (6 hours)

For the first segment, he identified several learning intentions. We will not repeat them all here, but here are a few of them:

- I am learning that an electric charge can be positive or negative.
- I am learning about the law of conservation of electric charge.
- I am learning to define *electric current*, *electrical potential difference* in a circuit, and *power*.
- I am learning to solve problems involving electric current, electric charge, and time.
- I am learning to solve problems involving electrical potential difference.

Of course, appropriate tasks will need to be aligned with each of these learning intentions. But that is for later, in Modules 6 and 7.

In distance learning, teachers share learning intentions with students in a variety of ways. For example,

- In an introduction to the New Testament course, the learning intentions were posted on the opening page in the learning management system and referenced at the start of each class meeting.

- In a cultural anthropology course, the learning intentions were posted in the chat box during a live session and reposted several times as tasks changed.

- In a cyber security course, the learning intentions were introduced at the outset of the video presentation and reviewed several times during the video.

Angie Hackman (Cuyamaca Community College, Biology) discusses how to explicitly share learning intentions and success criteria.

resources.corwin.com/ DLPlaybook-college

Graphic design professor Carlos Richards uses a distance learning log with ART 106 students in three-dimensional design. Based on the planning template, he and his colleagues worked together as a disciplinary program to identify learning intentions and success criteria (see Figure 5.2). A blank version of this is located in the appendix and is available for download (resources.corwin.com/DLPlaybook-college). Students save a copy of the document to their drives and track their progress across the week. For example, as part of a topic addressing the standard "Demonstrate a working knowledge of artistic methods, craft and formal structure as vehicles to enhance a solutions communicative value," students were focused on identifying artistic methods that add communicative value to their solutions. The learning intention was

- I am learning about the relationship between communicative value and specific method, craft, and formal structure.

The form includes success criteria, which we will explore in the next section. In addition, the form includes a space for students to record the tasks that they have completed relative to the learning intention. Dr. Richards uses "must-dos" and "may-dos" and students know that they can copy the tasks into their doc as they complete them. This allows Dr. Richards to monitor his students' progress and address needs that he identifies with small groups of students in synchronous learning sessions. He also provides his students with demonstrations via video that they can use on their own as well as examples of previously completed work.

There are a number of ways to create different types of learning intentions. For example, some are related to content and others are process related. Sometimes the learning is individual, and other times it is collective (more information can be found in *The Teacher Clarity Playbook*; Fisher, Frey, Amador, & Assof, 2019). For our purposes here, we'll focus on the individual learning of content, recognizing that professors will expand on this as their comfort with distance learning increases. At the very minimum, students should know what they are expected to learn for each task they are asked to do. In addition, students should know what success looks like, which brings us to success criteria.

Figure 5.2 Distance Learning Log

Student name:	Content: Communicative Value	Class: ART 106

Week of October 14

This Week's Learning Intention(s)	Tasks/Assessments I Completed
I am learning about the relationship between communicative value and specific method, craft, and formal structure.	

Success Criteria

Use the space below to rate your learning before and after each lesson.

Criteria	Before	After
I can explain craft and formal structure, with examples.		
I can describe different artistic methods used to enhance solutions communicative value.		
I can explain how craft and formal structure contribute to the communicative value of my solution.		
I can analyze the communicative value of my solution.		

IDENTIFY SUCCESS CRITERIA

The point of providing students success criteria is to ensure that they know what it means to have learned something. The effect size of success criteria is 0.54, making it another strong accelerator of student learning. There are many ways to ensure that students know what success looks like. In Dr. Richard's class, "I can" statements are used. In distance learning, we find these to be one of the useful ways professors can ensure that students know what learning looks like and can monitor their own progress. Of course, Dr. Richards does not simply list the success criteria on the form for students to download. He also talks about the success criteria in his opening video.

NOTE TO SELF

Let's practice. Based on the standard(s)/competencies you analyzed, what might be some learning intentions?

Concepts (nouns)	Skills (verbs)

Learning Intentions

1. _____

2. _____

3. _____

4. _____

5. _____

6. _____

7. _____

8. _____

Dr. Klein, the physics professor profiled earlier, also uses "I can" statements. The success criteria for the learning intentions presented earlier include the following:

Learning Intention	Success Criteria
I am learning that an electric charge can be positive or negative.	• I can recognize positive and negative charges. • I can summarize the difference between positive and negative charges.
I am learning about the law of conservation of electric charge.	• I can explain what the law of conservation of electric charge means for an isolated system. • I can define the law of conservation of electric charge in my own words. • I can write the law of conservation of electric charge.
I am learning to define *electric current, electrical potential difference* in a circuit, and *power*.	• I can describe (in my own words) *electric current, electrical potential difference* in a circuit, and *power*, and how they relate to each other. • I can recognize that electric current, electrical potential difference in a circuit, and power are related to circuits.
I am learning to solve problems involving electric current, electric charge, and time.	• I can determine values for current, electric charge, and time in complex situations. • I can recall that electric current is equal to the amount of charge movement per time. • I can calculate current in a simple circuit when charge is known and time is known.
I am learning to solve problems involving electrical potential difference.	• I can determine values for electrical potential difference in complex situations. • I can recall the formula for calculating electrical potential difference. • I can calculate the electrical potential difference between two points.

ITEMS ON A CHECKLIST NEED TO BE UNDERSTOOD BY STUDENTS.

In addition to "I can" statements, professors can use checklists, rubrics, exemplars, and modeling to ensure that students know what success looks like. In some content areas, these are more effective than "I can" statements. For example, in writing, the use of a checklist can help prevent formulaic pieces. Of course, items on a checklist need to be understood by students. Consider the following checklist for an introductory course in writing and rhetoric:

- Topic is introduced effectively.
- Related ideas are grouped together to give some organization.

- Topic is developed with multiple facts, definitions, or details.

- Linking words and phrases connect ideas within a category of information.

- There is a strong concluding statement or section.

- Sentences have clear and complete structure, with appropriate range and variety. Knowledge of writing language and conventions are shown.

- Any errors in usage do not interfere with meaning.

Of course, some of these are subjective. But "good" writing is hard to describe, and it takes practice and feedback to develop strong writing skills.

The students in writing professor Dr. Melanie Taylor's composition course used this checklist on a regular basis to improve their writing. Before they submitted a piece for peer review, they analyzed their own writing to identify areas that still needed work (and feedback) and areas that they believed were strong. Dr. Taylor also provided exemplars for students to analyze as mentor texts, some of which were strong examples and others that were not so effective. As Dr. Taylor notes, "It takes time, patience, and a lot of feedback to really improve writing. My students use the checklist as a self-assessment and then they use it to provide peer feedback. I also have individual writing conferences with students using video conferencing to talk through what I see. I ask them a lot of questions about the checklist so that they come to understand what success looks like. Sometimes, I share my screen and show them another piece of writing. I talk through what I see in this other piece so that they may be able to use it to improve their writing."

Note that Dr. Taylor used both a checklist and exemplars to ensure that her students understood what success looked like. She also modeled her thinking for some students as she read their papers. For example, while reading Nayeli's paper, Dr. Taylor said,

> Nayeli, the introduction of your paper reminds me of Andrew Clements, and we really like his writing. For me, as your reader, you really captured my attention right from the start. I'm wondering why you didn't think your introduction was effective, but we can come back to that in a minute. What I am noticing is that you present a fact and it was really interesting. But I noticed that it was just one fact. The checklist talks about multiple facts, definitions, or details. But I only see one. I'm thinking that you know more about this topic, especially from the power of your introduction. What are you thinking about now?

Their conversation continued, but note in this short snippet the ways in which Dr. Taylor modeled her thinking so that her student would develop a better understanding of what success looked like. Again, there is not one right way to ensure that students know what success looks like. We encourage you to try out different options and see which of them work for you. You will know you're successful when students know what learning looks like.

NOTE TO SELF

Let's practice. Based on the standard(s)/competencies you analyzed and the learning intentions you developed, what might be some success criteria?

Concepts (nouns)	Skills (verbs)

Success Criteria

1.

2.

3.

4.

5.

6.

7.

8.

FIND THE RELEVANCE

As we have noted before, boredom has a significantly negative impact on learning, with an effect size of –0.47. To counter that, professors need to make learning relevant for students. Students who have high levels of self-regulation tend of find relevance in a lot of the learning they're introduced to. Students who have low levels of self-regulation need help finding relevance. What is relevant to one person may not be relevant to another. Priniski, Hecht, and Harackiewicz (2018) conceptualize relevance across a continuum from least to most relevant. We have defined these as follows:

- **Personal association** is through a connection to an object or memory, such as enjoying a reading about Costa Rica because the student was born there before immigrating to the United States. Similarly, association occurs when a student makes a connection with something outside the classroom and thus wants to learn more.

- **Personal usefulness** is derived from a student's belief that a task or text will help them reach a personal goal. For example, a student reads a series of articles about the political definitions of *justice* and *injustice* to better understand the history the development of these definitions. Or a student perseveres through a mathematics course because she believes that the knowledge will help her gain admission to a specific graduate program in mechanical engineering.

- **Personal identification** is the most motivating type of relevancy and stems from a deep understanding that the task or text aligns with one's identity. When students get to learn about themselves, their problem solving, and their ability to impact others, relevance is increased. For example, a student who wants to build shelters for stray cats is highly motivated to learn geometry. A student who sees herself as a poet seeks feedback and lessons about voice, ideas, and organization.

Alice Hevener, an English professor, knows that her students are generally engaged in their learning. They like learning about how themes from classic literature are prevalent in today's society and culture (i.e., *Canterbury Tales, Things Fall Apart, Their Eyes Were Watching God, Love in the Time of Cholera*). When she introduces a new text to her students, she asks them why we focus on specific characters in these novels, short stories, or poems. The range of responses on a given day included

- Because when we see how characters feel we understand why they do things
- Because characters help us think about our behavior
- Because characters have emotions that reflect the culture in which they were written

Similarly, the students in Linda Craddick's HTH 325 epidemiology course find relevance in their lessons when she talks with them about why they are learning

Mathew Mansoor (Cuyamaca Community College, Psychology) shares ways to make learning relevant from a distance.

resources.corwin.com/ DLPlaybook-college

certain things. She tries to make connections with students' experiences. For example, when looking at ways in which variance in disease occurrence is documented, she uses real case studies with data from the Centers for Disease Control and Prevention. Dr. Craddick regularly made connections to healthy living on college and university campuses as well as the aspirations of students (e.g., their future careers).

CONCLUSION

Teacher clarity is an important consideration in developing distance learning opportunities for students. We can't forget that students in *any* learning environment need to know what they are learning and how they will know if they are successful. Further, addressing the relevance of the lesson can engage students. We'll spend more time on engagement in the next module.

Teacher clarity is more than learning intentions and success criteria, as we will explore further in this book. But they are important components for ensuring that students learn. The learning intentions and success criteria are derived from the standards or competencies and teacher-made decisions about the effective flow of information for students' learning. As a final task for this module, now that you have a sense of the value of teacher credibility, complete the following self-assessment.

FACTOR	USING THE "TRAFFIC LIGHT" SCALE, EVALUATE YOUR CURRENT LEVEL OF IMPLEMENTATION (GREEN IS GOOD OR REGULARLY; RED IS THE OPPOSITE).	USING THE SCALE BELOW, DETERMINE HOW IMPORTANT THIS FACTOR IS FOR YOU.
Analyzing standards		not at all somewhat very extremely
Developing learning units and flowing lessons		not at all somewhat very extremely
Creating learning intentions		not at all somewhat very extremely
Identifying success criteria		not at all somewhat very extremely
Finding relevance		not at all somewhat very extremely

MODULE 6

ENGAGING TASKS AT A DISTANCE

Engagement is at the core of learning. Disengaged students learn less and are often negatively labeled as "unmotivated" or "a problem." Without question, a disengaged learner may well be a bored one. With an effect size of −0.47, boredom is a powerful decelerator to student learning. Many of us have witnessed this firsthand in virtual learning sessions as students switch off microphones and cameras in order to turn their attention to something else. However, we wonder to what extent the achievement gap discussed in policy papers and faculty meetings is really an engagement gap.

Gauging student engagement is more than just cataloging who is turning in their assignments or leaning forward in their seats with eyes on the professor (i.e., playing school). Engagement has historically been understood across three dimensions: behavioral, cognitive, and emotional engagement (Fredricks, Blumenfeld, & Paris, 2004). It turns out that these are too interrelated and thus are not very predictive of student success. Of course, if a student is sleeping, they can't engage. Following this review of a historical model of engagement, we'll turn to a more compelling model that presents engagement along a continuum, which we find more compelling from a learning perspective.

Behavioral engagement is the dimension most commonly referenced when describing a student's engagement. These are observable academic actions that professors instantly recognize. Two items are a student's level of participation in class and submission of assignments. But behavioral engagement alone is an insufficient gauge. We perceive students who know how to "do school" in online and face-to-face classrooms as engaged. But Windschitl (2019) defines *doing school* as "rote and shallow learning performances, which students and teachers give to each other to signify that they are accomplishing normative classroom tasks" (p. 8).

Cognitive engagement provides further nuance to what it means to be engaged with learning. Now we're talking about the psychological effort students exert to

MANY OF US HAVE WITNESSED THIS FIRSTHAND . . . AS STUDENTS SWITCH OFF MICROPHONES AND CAMERAS IN ORDER TO TURN THEIR ATTENTION TO SOMETHING ELSE.

master content. Students who seek challenge and self-regulate are said to be cognitively engaged. Observable actions include

- Planning

- Monitoring their own progress

- Setting goals

- Solving problems

Emotional engagement is the *affective* dimension of learning. Interest and relationships contribute to a student's ability to learn. Learners who have a sense of belonging and have an affinity toward classmates are more likely to

- Engage in discussions

- Pose questions

- Seek help when needed

- Exhibit curiosity about a subject

Marisol Thayre (Cuyamaca Community College, English) explains the importance of engaging learners from a distance.

resources.corwin.com/ DLPlaybook-college

We invite you to activate your prior knowledge about how you address each dimension instructionally and in your curricular design.

Amy Berry (2020) interviewed teachers about the conception of engagement, and most often they saw engagement more in terms of "doing." The focus seemed to be whether or not the students engaged in doing the task. Of course, we can have observable cues of students engaging in doing tasks. Berry called this *participating*, but many professors want more. This led to her model with three forms of engagement and three of disengagement. According to Berry, students can move between these forms. Naturally, we all want to help students move from participating or "doing" to investing and driving their own learning (see Figure 6.1).

Figure 6.1 A Continuum of Engagement

ACTIVE ⟵————————————— PASSIVE ————————————⟶ ACTIVE

Disrupting	Avoiding	Withdrawing	Participating	Investing	Driving
Distracting others Disrupting the learning	Looking for ways to avoid work Off-task behavior	Being distracted Physically separating from group	Doing work Paying attention Responding to questions	Asking questions Valuing the learning	Setting goals Seeking feedback Self-assessment

DISENGAGEMENT	ENGAGEMENT

DRAWING ON MY EXPERTISE

What instructional techniques and curricular design approaches do you use to engage students in each dimension?

	INSTRUCTIONAL TECHNIQUES	CURRICULAR DESIGN
Behavioral engagement		
Cognitive engagement		
Emotional engagement		

THINK FUNCTIONS OF ENGAGEMENT, NOT JUST TOOLS

It can be intimidating to keep track of all the technology tools available for use by teachers and students in a distance learning environment. Educators around the world experienced this anxiety to varying degrees in the rapid move to distance and remote learning in 2020. As we scrambled to find ways to re-create our classrooms in a distance environment, the focus in many cases was on the tools themselves. How to install and operate took precedence over whether these tools were actually useful to teachers and students. In fact, many of the professional learning workshops available for faculty are still all about the tools and not the teaching. So, let's take a deep breath and recall what it is that students need to be able to accomplish in their learning (Frey, Fisher, & Gonzalez, 2013, p. 1):

- *Find information* efficiently and be able to evaluate whether the information is useful, credible, accurate, and corroborated by other sources.

- *Use information* accurately and ethically.

- *Create information* such that its creation deepens one's understanding.

- *Share information* responsibly with audiences for a variety of purposes.

As noted previously, it isn't the medium that matters. Information is manipulated verbally, with paper and pencil, and through interpretive dance, for that matter. A collaboratively constructed document by a group of students could happen with a chart paper and a handful of markers, or it could occur online using web-based software. These functions transcend the spaces in which they are enacted and serve as a foundation for thinking about the ways to engage learners. You won't find a long list of web-based tools in this playbook, as innovative ones seem to blossom weekly. By shifting the attention from the tools (which are cool and seemingly infinite) to the *functions*, we can hone what we need to accomplish in order to build students' capacity in face-to-face and distance learning.
The functions of learning lead right back to the engagement in learning (see Figure 6.2 for examples).

Figure 6.2 Functions and Tools

	Engagement Opportunities	Sample Tools
Finding Information	• Can locate information sources • Can organize and analyze information sources for accuracy and utility to the task • Locating information is driven by curiosity	• Google • Kahoot • MindMeister Add-On • Padlet • Quizlet • Twitter
Using Information	• Can cite sources of information • Makes judgments about how best to use information • Asks questions the information provokes	• Evernote • Flipgrid • Grammarly • PlayPosit
Creating Information	• Can write and discuss information according to grade-level expectations • Transforms information in order to explore ideas new to the learner • Takes academic risks to innovate	• Google Docs • ThingLink • TikTok • Turnitin
Sharing Information	• Accurately matches purpose to audience • Uses metacognitive thinking to identify the best strategies for the stated purpose • Is resourceful and resilient	• Animoto • Remind • Storybird • Tikok • WeVideo • YouTube

Josh Streeter (James Madison University, Theater and Dance) talks tools for supporting learner engagement.

resources.corwin.com/ DLPlaybook-college

SET THE CONDITIONS FOR ENGAGEMENT AND LEARNING

Astute faculty know that all that is taught is not necessarily learned, regardless of the setting. The quest, then, is to determine what ingredients are vital for learning to occur. We ask ourselves, what is the right combination of experiences that ensure learning? What conditions must be present? Faculty members whose mission it is to cultivate engaged learners teach the kinds of strategies learners need and create opportunities for students to use them. They hold a metaphorical mirror up to students to promote reflection, self-questioning, problem solving, and decision-making. These professors mediate the thinking of their students as often as they possibly can, so that their students can gain more insight into how and when they learn and associate their actions to results. And they possess a clear vision of the kind of learner they are building because they know the characteristics of an engaged learner: behaviorally, cognitively, and emotionally.

SELECT THE TOOLS THAT MEET THESE FUNCTIONS AND CONDITIONS

LET'S TAKE A DEEP BREATH AND RECALL WHAT IT IS THAT STUDENTS NEED TO BE ABLE TO ACCOMPLISH IN THEIR LEARNING.

Selecting a limited suite of tools can be challenging, as there are so many to choose from. We will confess that we have seen too many endless lists of tools and resources to scroll through. However, they don't also offer guidance in how to curate a manageable number of tools that will address the learning functions you need to optimize engagement levels. Here are some considerations as you make decisions on which tools make the most sense for your context. Many learning management systems (LMS) come with built-in tools, which doesn't mean you need to use them all. In addition, school districts have their own guidelines about how external tools can be utilized, and under what conditions. Having said that, here are some questions for consideration, whether examining LMS built-in tools or those that are on external sites (see Figure 6.3). You can find additional copies of this template on this book's companion website (resources.corwin.com/DLPlaybook-college).

Some of the questions you should consider include the following:

- What learning function does this tool fulfill?

- Does the tool support thinking and doing that aligns with the learning intentions and success criteria for the class meeting or task?

- Can the students use the tool with minimal assistance? If not, are there resources available through the libraries or instructional technology to support learners?

- How will learners with limited access to the Internet engage with this tool? Are there alternatives that achieve the same learning function?

- Does this tool have accessibility features that are aligned to digital compliance requirements (e.g., provides closed captioning, supports screen-reader software)? What are they?

Susan Almarode (University of Virginia, Nursing) talks tools that serve specific functions and conditions.

resources.corwin.com/ DLPlaybook-college

NOTE TO SELF

What conditions are necessary in order to perform these functions in face-to-face classrooms? In distance learning?

	FACE-TO-FACE CLASSROOMS	DISTANCE LEARNING CLASSROOMS
Finding Information		
Using Information		
Creating Information		
Sharing Information		

Figure 6.3 Evaluation of Distance Learning Tools

Name of Tool _____

Question	Answer
What learning function does this tool fulfill?	
Does the tool support thinking and doing that aligns with the learning intentions and success criteria for the class meeting or task?	
Can the students use the tool with minimal assistance? If not, are there resources available through the libraries or instructional technology to support learners?	
How will learners with limited access to the Internet engage with this tool? Are there alternatives that achieve the same learning function?	
Does this tool have accessibility features that are aligned to digital compliance requirements (e.g., provides closed captioning, supports screen-reader software)? What are they?	
Key Features Checklist ☐ A way to prerecord lessons and directions ☐ A written or video-based discussion forum for students ☐ A means for students to submit work ☐ A way to provide feedback to students about their work ☐ A way for students to provide feedback to one another ☐ Assessment tools that allow for formative and summative evaluation ☐ A way to host individual meetings with students, families, and other professionals ☐ A way to share and communicate with other teachers	

In addition, you need productivity tools that allow you to perform major teaching functions. Again, many LMS platforms offer features for grading online and such. In addition, Figure 6.3 includes a key features checklist. You don't necessarily need all of the functions listed on the checklist, but they are aspects you may want to consider.

Our point is that you will want to avoid overwhelming your students and yourself with too many tools. Select them judiciously; better yet, select them as departments, majors, or programs so there is consistency for students and collegial support for you. Introduce and teach the tools you have selected such that you aren't clustering them too closely together. After all, you wouldn't teach students everything they need to know about your classroom on the very first day. Think judiciously and phase in the tools you'll be using so you aren't overwhelming your students' capacity or yours.

A virtual Bitmoji classroom is an interactive space for students to click hyperlinks to resources, such as websites, documents, lessons, assignments. Richard Conley, a geology professor, noted, "I would like to know about this, but I thought, is it difficult and will it take a lot of time? Or is it just a cutesy thing that doesn't hold value? I decided that my virtual classroom will be a shell in which I can easily change the content, and that's what makes it a fun and informative way to deliver digital learning instruction."

Dr. Conley continues, "I wanted to provide a space to hold resources needed for learners' capstone presentation format called PechaKucha, which uses a 20 × 20 format to tell a story or research visually, with 20 slides and 20 seconds of one's own commentary (PechaKucha 20×20, n.d.)." He created this in Google Slides. It has an introduction with screencasting that orients students to new content, which is the PechaKucha presentation format, and how to use it (Chen, Vargas, Thompson, & Carter, 2014). He then used Loom for screencasts to make the content easily accessible and provide a visually interesting presentation. Loom is free, cloud based, and easy to edit. All resources are located in the virtual bookcase through hyperlinks. The hyperlink to PechaKucha CREATE is the tool/video that demonstrates how to produce this type of presentation, and in the bookcase are PDF links for the assessment rubric and tips for this type of presentation format. Additionally, there are resources with hyperlinks to Splash and Pixabay for free quality images to support their visual research story and another one for Canva, which allows students to create infographics or design posters to further support their message. Dr. Conley says, "I also included a PechaKucha example that informs the students of why and how to create great slides. My virtual classroom was converted from Google Slides into a pdf and then uploaded to Canvas. Ultimately, my virtual classroom delivers a flexible, accessible, and motivating online environment."

Now it is your turn to itemize what you have and what you need for your distance classroom. We will use the analogy of being an effective grocery shopper. You make a weekly list of the meals you'll prepare, then do a scan of your pantry and refrigerator to see how much you have and what you will need. Every shopper has a budget, so get what you need and resist the urge to fill your cart up too full.

NOTE TO SELF

Scan your virtual classroom tools: What will students need? What will you need?

	YES	NOT YET	DON'T NEED
Video recording for lessons and directions			
Discussion forum for students			
Student work submission			
Feedback tool			
Formative and summative evaluation			
Individual meeting platform			
Sharing professional learning with colleagues			

DESIGN TASKS WITH ENGAGEMENT IN MIND

The tasks students complete, whether synchronously or asynchronously, should foster learning. Tasks that are busy work, keeping hands busy but minds turned off, are not going to deliver the kind of learning that keeps students engaged, moving from doing to driving as Berry (2020) would put it. Too often students are asked to do an inordinate amount of rote learning with little rationale for why the learning is occurring. Practice is important, of course, and students need to memorize information in order to perform more challenging tasks. Unfortunately, too many online tasks seem to be focused on recall and recognition tasks at the expense of other kinds of learning.

Katie Dawson (University of Texas at Austin, Theater and Dance) describes what makes an authentic task from a distance.

resources.corwin.com/ DLPlaybook-college

Learning remotely doesn't need to be reduced to completing endless amounts of worksheets. The tasks students complete in the company of one another or independently have the potential of fostering engagement through thoughtful design. The South Australia Department for Education and Child Development (2019) supports teachers through professional learning geared toward making tasks more engaging in order to deepen learning. Their recommendations transcend settings:

- **Encourage students to think in more than one way by transforming from closed to open tasks.** Examine the task by looking for ways students can enter from more than one entry point or by considering more than one perspective. For example, pose problems to students that can be solved in multiple ways.

- **Move from information to understanding by requiring students to connect and relate.** Design some tasks so that students need to compare and contrast two phenomena, identify rules and patterns, and figure out when seemingly dissimilar ideas are actually related.

- **Ask students what they think first, rather than telling them what they will need.** Create tasks that allow students to try out their ideas first to see what works and what doesn't. For instance, ask students what might work best to resolve a problem, such as a design-based thinking task in engineering.

- **Position students to plan a way forward by moving from procedure to problem solving.** Foster a group's reliance on one another by providing them insufficient information at first, giving them only some of the steps, or including some irrelevant information.

Tasks designed with these principles in mind can increase engagement, whether performed independently or in collaboration with others.

NOTE TO SELF

Use the task design principles to match to four different online tasks you currently use.

An open task

An understanding task

An asking task

A problem-solving task

DESIGN A CONSIDERATE SCHEDULE TO PROMOTE ENGAGEMENT

Professors and students have experienced the "Zoom exhaustion" that comes from too many hours trying to sit still and remain engaged in front of a screen. Some colleges and universities initially tried to replicate their classes in real time using schedules that were designed for face-to-face instruction. They quickly found out that five or six hours of daily instruction, complete with the same class schedules, was not workable. One reason is because life in our homes and apartments doesn't run on the college or university schedule, and the burden placed on students, roommates, and families made it nearly impossible for them to manage a school– or work–life balance.

The time we are in front of students in live sessions should be prioritized for connection, discussion, and interaction. That means that some learning should occur asynchronously, rather than in real time. When planning class meetings, think about learning experiences students need to prepare them for the interactive discussions you host in a virtual setting. These might be readings, short videos for students to preview, or written tasks that leverage prior knowledge.

Consistency and predictability of schedule are student and family friendly. Design weekly schedules that provide students with expectations about tasks to be accomplished before and after live sessions. Be sure to include the learning intentions, success criteria, and any assessments so that students have a clear sense of purpose and can ask questions in advance. Sociology professor Karen Blauch provides her students with digital sticky notes to sort as teams. In preparation for an assessment, teams sorted them according to their level of confidence, which allowed her to use targeted reteaching as needed (see Figure 6.4).

A scheduling template for the learning can help tremendously in providing students with consistent and predictable ways to engage with the content, with you and with their peers. A template such as the one in Figure 6.4 is particularly useful for multiple courses in a semester and for students who are meeting with several professors over the course of a semester. It's not that students complete all of the tasks at the bottom of the page, but rather that they know when they are responsible for which things.

Nancy Jones (San Diego State University, Business) shares video cartoons as a way to engage learners.

resources.corwin.com/ DLPlaybook-college

One mistake we made early on was in not giving attention to conflicting schedules. We quickly realized that while professors were doing their best to schedule class meetings, study sessions, and virtual or remote office hours, the result was that students, roommates, and families couldn't possibly juggle meetings that changed each day. And what is a student supposed to do when their English professor and biology professor were unknowingly asking for the same time? We shifted to specific days of the week so that live sessions for each subject are evenly spaced. Just as a class schedule is useful to all of us while on campus and in academic halls, so is a scheduling template in a distance learning environment.

A schedule that is inconsistent and unpredictable is going to provoke behavioral disengagement. Think back to the indicators we outlined at the beginning of this module:

- Participating in college or university functions

- Attending and participating in class activities and discussions

- Following college and university policies

- Studying

- Completing assignments

There are students who have difficulty doing this in face-to-face classrooms. But how much organizational structure do we provide for those students? It is even more important when students are at a distance and the interactions are in virtual spaces.

Figure 6.4 Distance Learning Weekly Planner

Class: _____   Content: _____

Week of (DATE) _____

This Week's Learning Targets/Intentions	Tasks/Assessments	Success Criteria
I am learning		I can

Monday	Tuesday	Wednesday	Thursday	Friday
Attend	Attend	Attend	Attend	Attend
Read	Read	Read	Read	Read
Watch	Watch	Watch	Watch	Watch
Discuss	Discuss	Discuss	Discuss	Discuss
Turn in	Turn in	Turn in	Turn in	Turn in

What scheduling issues are you taking into consideration at your college or university? What about within your department or program of study?

When will you hold synchronous sessions? How frequently? For how long?	
How will asynchronous learning bracket live sessions (before and after)?	
What do students need in order to be supportive (but not to burden them with doing school themselves)?	
How will students access technology help?	
How will you collect student questions and concerns?	
How will you coordinate your efforts with other faculty members?	

CONCLUSION

The next normal in postsecondary education requires that we build the capacity of our students and ourselves to shift fluidly between mediums in order to keep learning moving forward. This can be partially accomplished in face-to-face classrooms using blended learning approaches. However, in order to foster our collective capacity in all settings, we need to proactively consider these functions and the conditions that support them across platforms and foreground them with intention. As a final task for this module, self-assess to rank factors related to engagement. This will allow you to target your professional learning efforts.

FACTOR	USING THE "TRAFFIC LIGHT" SCALE, EVALUATE YOUR CURRENT LEVEL OF IMPLEMENTATION (GREEN IS GOOD OR REGULARLY; RED IS THE OPPOSITE).	USING THE SCALE BELOW, DETERMINE HOW IMPORTANT THIS FACTOR IS FOR YOU.
Gauging dimensions of engagement		not at all — somewhat — very — extremely
Thinking functions, not just tools		not at all — somewhat — very — extremely
Setting the conditions for engagement and learning		not at all — somewhat — very — extremely
Selecting the tools that meet these functions and conditions		not at all — somewhat — very — extremely
Designing tasks with engagement in mind		not at all — somewhat — very — extremely
Designing a considerate schedule to promote engagement		not at all — somewhat — very — extremely
Greeting students		not at all — somewhat — very — extremely
Learning students' names and how to pronounce them		not at all — somewhat — very — extremely
Learning about their interests		not at all — somewhat — very — extremely

MODULE 7

PLANNING LEARNING EXPERIENCES AT A DISTANCE

LEARNING INTENTIONS

- I am learning to design experiences that impact students' understanding.

- I am learning how various strategies align with different aspects of distance learning.

SUCCESS CRITERIA

- I can identify high-leverage instructional strategies that are likely to impact students' learning.

- I can adjust instructional experiences when students are not learning.

- I can demonstrate necessary aspects of learning for students.

- I can design collaborative tasks that are appropriately challenging.

- I can coach and facilitate students' learning based on the needs I have identified.

- I can design practice that is both spaced and deliberate.

We care about student learning and believe that there is no one right way to teach. If students are learning at least one year of content for each year in school, we're happy. We believe too much talk has focused on teaching and not enough on learning. Having said that, educators do need to design meaningful learning experiences that provide students with opportunities to learn. As we have noted before, teachers should not hold an instructional strategy in higher esteem than their students' learning. Thus, this module focuses on a framework for instruction, and we provide examples of instructional routines that teachers might find useful. Importantly, these are examples. If they do not work for your students, please change them.

Kim Lin, a professor of justice studies, is introducing a semester-long book club for his senior seminar students (JUST 450). As part of this book club, he wanted students to do the following as part of his learning intentions:

- Identify a contemporary problem in justice studies.

- Develop and support a workable solution to the problem (individually and as a group).

Dr. Lin created a video in which he talked about the process for identifying a contemporary problem and then forming a book club around that problem. This involves selecting titles that explore that problem from multiple perspectives. Students then voted on the book that they would like to read. He created groups and students scheduled times to meet with their groups

to talk about their readings. The sessions were recorded for Dr. Lin to review, but he regularly joined the groups to guide and facilitate their discussions. Students were asked to respond to daily writing prompts to practice their composing of a workable solution, and Dr. Lin provided students feedback on their responses. The final essay focused on developing and supporting a workable solution. Students used information from their text and their own experiences to complete the task. The students would load their responses into the class learning management systems, which provided the opportunity for two peers to review their papers before Dr. Lin used a rubric to assign them a score.

The decisions that Dr. Lin made instructionally worked for him and impacted his students' learning as evidenced by their proposed solutions, measured on a rubric. Dr. Lin monitors progress across the semester to see the impact of the book club on students' thinking. But the individual strategies are less important. What is more important is the framework that guides his decision-making. Did you notice that Dr. Lin provided clear instructions? He also ensured that his students had opportunities to collaborate. Further, he facilitated and coached the thinking of his students and provided them with opportunities to practice. And all of this was based on what he wanted students to learn, the learning intentions and success criteria, or purpose for learning. Figure 7.1 contains a visual of the instructional framework that guides the design of lessons.

Figure 7.1   Instructional Framework

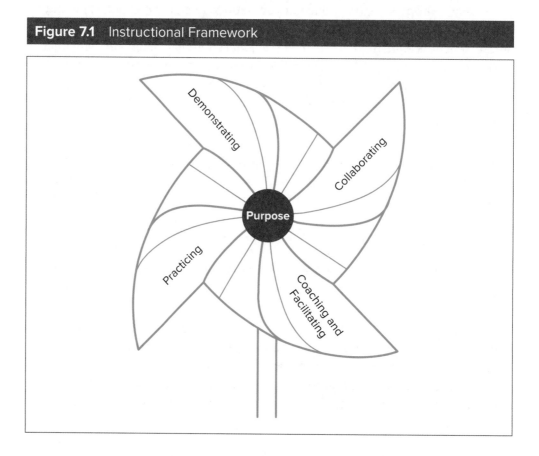

DRAWING ON MY EXPERTISE

Consider the following questions about your past experiences with quality instruction.

1. How do I provide students input and information?

2. How do I structure collaborative tasks?

3. How do I guide students' thinking?

4. How do I ensure students practice and apply what they have learned?

As you may have noticed, the center of the pinwheel is the purpose or intention for learning. As we noted in Module 5, teacher clarity plays a significant role in students' learning. In fact, it drives the instructional decisions that professors make. The tasks students are assigned must be aligned with the goal for learning. Also, the purpose for learning helps professors make decisions about how to use instructional minutes. Thus, all of the other parts of the pinwheel metaphorically spin around the pin in the middle, which is the purpose.

In planning for distance learning, unlike a traditional class meeting for which there is a set time, professors must consider the various ways and times that students will access the content, skills, and understandings of the class. In some cases, there are synchronous and asynchronous learning opportunities spread across a week. In other cases, there are daily expectations for students. As you think about your plan, consider the strategic use of each of the four blades (or aspects) of the pinwheel: demonstrating, collaborating, coaching and facilitating, and practicing. Below, we will delve into each of these aspects more deeply.

WHAT IS MOST IMPORTANT IS THE FRAMEWORK THAT GUIDES YOUR DECISION-MAKING.

DEMONSTRATING

Demonstrations provide students with examples of what they will do or learn. This aspect of learning provides students with a glimpse inside the mind of another person. Often this is the professor, but it does not have to be. For example, a nursing student in his clinical applications and reasoning class recorded a time-lapse video of him using the patient simulator to provide acute clinical care and narrated the final version, sharing his thinking about what he was doing over that span of time. This demonstration provided other students with an example that they could use as they completed their own simulations. The point was not to reproduce what they saw in the video as the one shared by the student demonstrating, but rather to climb inside his mind and understand his thinking.

The tasks students are assigned must BE aligned with the goal for learning.

There are a number of ways that teachers can demonstrate for students:

- Direct instruction

- Think-alouds and think-alongs

- Worked examples

- Lectures

- Share sessions

Each of these approaches allows the person demonstrating to share their thinking with others. Just showing someone how to do something does not ensure that they can do it later. How many times have you seen someone cut hair, change a tire, or bake a cake, and you are still not sure you can do it yourself? Imagine the

Marisol Thayre (Cuyamaca Community College, English) discusses modeling and teaching during remote instruction.

resources.corwin.com/ DLPlaybook-college

difference if someone shared the thinking involved in each step of the process (and then allowed you to practice and receive feedback). That might just make the difference for you to be able to own that learning.

Thinking is invisible. A major aim in classes is to help make this thinking more visible such as by using these four methods. Our cognitive processes become apparent to others primarily when we speak or write. Many of the concepts and skills we teach are abstract. Sharing thinking with students allows them a glimpse into the inner workings of our brains as we process and act upon information. The research world calls this a *think-aloud*, but we worry that this term focuses exclusively on the teacher, so we like to use the phrase *think-along* to ensure that students are engaged in the process as their teachers think aloud.

THINK-ALONGS

Our experience has been that off-the-cuff think-alongs tend to be unfocused and can leave students more confused. A planned think-along ensures a higher degree of clarity. Resist the urge to clutter your think-alongs with too many divergent ideas—it shouldn't be a stream of consciousness. We used the following guidelines (Fisher, Frey, & Lapp, 2009) to plan and record robust think-alongs about a passage from George Orwell's *Animal Farm* that we recorded for students to view (and view again, if needed):

- **Name the strategy, skill, or task.** "I'm going to think out loud about how I noticed repetition in this passage."

- **State the purpose of the strategy, skill, or task.** "Good speakers who are giving a speech will often repeat a key idea or two again and again. It makes the message stick."

- **Explain when the strategy or skill is used.** "The first thing that got me noticing that there was going to be some repetition coming was in the first line of the first paragraph: 'And remember, comrades.' Major is telling the other animals that something important is coming next because he is telling them that this is going to be something important to remember."

- **Use analogies to link prior knowledge to new learning.** "It's like when I see a politician giving a speech at a rally. They have a slogan and they repeat it over and over so you remember it long after the speech is over."

- **Demonstrate how the skill, strategy, or task is completed.** "I'm going to show you the repetition I saw in the first paragraph. First, he says, 'Never listen. . . .' Then he says, 'It is all lies.' Then at the end of the paragraph he says again, 'All men are enemies. All animals are comrades.' Three times in one paragraph he repeats the same idea: Don't listen to Man. He can't be trusted. All Men are the enemy.' I noticed this because the repetition was so close together."

- **Alert learners to errors to avoid.** "Speakers can use repetition pretty effectively, but I know I have to be on the lookout for how a repeated message can change. It's like the telephone game when you whisper a

PLANNING

message to one person, who then whispers it to another. By the time it gets back to the first person, the message is completely different. I look for repetition, but I also have to keep an eye out for how the message might change when other speakers use it."

- **Assess the use of the skill.** "So, I'm going to make a note in the margin that there is some repetition happening, and I am going to highlight those sentences where I saw it happening. I want to be able to come back to the original message to compare it if others use a similar message. I want to be able to see if it has stayed the same or if it has changed."

A planning tool for think-alongs can be found in Figure 7.2. Think-alongs, as with most other forms of demonstrating, are delivered using first-person language. This spoken language mirrors one's own internal dialogue. These "I" statements can feel awkward at first, but they contribute to a think-along's effectiveness by triggering empathetic listening on the part of the student. It is human nature to respond emotionally to such statements. The use of "I" statements invites students into the thinking process in ways that second-person directives do not. Consider the difference between the two:

- **First-person statement:** "When I read this term, I'm confused so I scan back up to the bolded definition in the previous paragraph to remind myself what it means."

- **Second-person statement:** "When you run into an unfamiliar term, remember to scan back up and reread the bolded definition."

The first example gives students insight into the use of a comprehension strategy as it is deployed during the act of reading. The second, while good advice, uncouples the strategy from the decision to use it. Novice learners don't just need to know what the strategy is—they need to know when to apply it.

This approach is also very helpful in STEM disciplines. Physics professor Natalie Coltfield uses think-alongs to model how learners should approach and work through problems. "I also use them to model the type of thinking that should be used to decide the type of problem and then the best approach to solving that problem. Plus, my students can go back and watch these videos again as a way to review."

JUST SHOWING SOMEONE HOW TO DO SOMETHING DOES NOT ENSURE THAT THEY CAN DO IT LATER.

DIRECT INSTRUCTION

Direct instruction is another way to demonstrate for students. To be sure, direct instruction has gotten a bad rap in some quarters. In fact, it might be one of the most misunderstood instructional approaches out there. And to be quite honest, we are probably to blame for that misunderstanding by relying so heavily on lecture. Impressions about direct instruction usually cluster into three categories:

1. It is scripted and didactic.

2. It is inflexible.

3. It devalues teacher judgment.

Figure 7.2 Think-Along Planning Template

Component	Places in the Text and Language to Be Used
Name the strategy, skill, or task.	
State the purpose of the strategy, skill, or task.	
Explain when the strategy or skill is used.	
Use analogies to link prior knowledge to new learning.	
Demonstrate how the skill, strategy, or task is completed.	
Alert learners to errors to avoid.	
Assess the use of the skill.	

With an effect size of 0.59, direct instruction offers a pedagogical pathway that provides students with the modeling, scaffolding, and practice they require when learning new skills and concepts. Rosenshine (2008) noted that the structure of a direct instruction lesson should follow a pattern that includes the following:

1. Begin a learning experience with a short review of previous learning. Going from the known to the new is powerful.

2. Begin a lesson with a short statement of goals (e.g., learning intentions and success criteria).

3. Present new material in small steps, providing practice for students after each step. This is where developing a learning progression is so important.

4. Give clear and detailed instructions and explanations.

5. Provide a high level of active practice for all students.

6. Ask a large number of questions, check for student understanding, and obtain responses from all students.

7. Guide students during initial practice.

8. Provide explicit instruction and practice exercises; monitor students during these practice exercises.

WORKED EXAMPLES

A **worked example** is a math problem that has been fully completed to show each step of a mathematician's arrival at a solution. These have been shown to be useful for students in completing problems more efficiently and accurately and have an effect size of 0.37. It is important, of course, to identify from the beginning whether a worked example is correct or erroneous. Worked examples that are erroneous as well as those that are correct can spark student thinking as they hypothesize why the mathematician made the decisions they did to arrive at a solution. Worked examples are not limited to use in mathematics. Teachers can share their thinking about writing, art, lab reports, and many other worked examples. Essentially, the professor (or another student) thinks aloud about an example that has already been completed using "I" statements as we noted before. The goal is to share your thinking and develop students' mental models so that they incorporate that type of thinking into their own practices.

Another advantage of using worked examples is that they help reduce the cognitive load on students. Remember most of us struggle to remember more than four to six things at once, our working memory is limited, and we want students to focus on the most important parts of the lesson and not be distracted by the lesser important parts. As we show worked examples, there can be a "expertise reversal effect" as students start by listening to explicit instruction and dialogue from the teacher and begin to incorporate this thinking and explanations as part of their own skills and conversion to longer-term memory. They can hear the problem solving and reduce their focus on the redundant parts; this is also the core of the gradual release of responsibility by the professor.

UNFORTUNATELY, THERE ARE MANY CLASSROOMS IN WHICH TEACHERS DO ALMOST ALL OF THE TALKING. ONE OF THE RISKS WITH DISTANCE LEARNING IS THAT TEACHERS REPLICATE ALL OF THAT TALK ONLINE.

Joseph Assof (Cuyamaca Community College, Mathematics) talks about moving tasks online.

resources.corwin.com/ DLPlaybook-college

How can I use direct instruction in my distance learning classes?

What concept or skill do my students need?

What is the goal for the lesson?

How can I explain this to students?

How can I ensure that they practice as I observe?

How can I teach them so they can then teach others?

LECTURES

Of course, professors can also record their **lectures** and demonstrate their content knowledge for students. Lectures should not go on and on, especially in a virtual environment, and should include opportunities to check for understanding. Successful use of lectures in a virtual environment often includes an integrated quiz feature in video lectures to check students' understanding along the way. When they answer incorrectly, the system requires that they re-watch the section and answer again.

SHARE SESSIONS

Professors can use **share sessions** in which we visually show students how to do something. For example, Jackie Neyland, a kinesiology professor, provides share sessions with her students in KIN 100: Lifetime Fitness. Students engage in yoga with Dr. Neyland so that they can learn, practice, and implement lifetime fitness habits alongside their professor.

COLLABORATING

One of the mindframes we value is "I engage as much in dialogue as monologue." Unfortunately, there are many classrooms in which professors do almost all of the talking. One of the risks with distance learning is that professors replicate all of that talk online or even increase the amount of talk so that they can fill the space. But the second aspect noted in our pinwheel of instruction is **collaborating**. We believe that students should be provided time to engage in dialogue with their peers. And we believe that these dialogues between and among students are powerful ways to improve learning. In fact, the effect size for classroom discussion is 0.82. These meta-analyses do not include evidence from online discussions, but we think that the same rules generally apply. For example, the task has to be complex enough to warrant more than one person. Further, students need to believe that their groups will impact their collective and individual learning and seek evidence of the impact of their efforts.

An important consideration is when to invite students to dialogue with the professor and with each other. We recommend that they do so once they have acquired sufficient knowledge and begin to grapple with the relations between ideas. That's the ideal time to ask them to take more ownership or regulate their own learning. This is when the power of listening to others, thinking aloud themselves, and querying, justifying, exploring, and being curious are most successful.

There are a number of routines that have been tested in physical classrooms that professors are adapting for distance learning. These include text rendering, jigsaw, and reciprocal teaching. Of course, there are many other collaborative routines that can be used in distance learning, not to mention a wide range of tools, such as Google Docs, Sheets, and Slides, that allow students to interact with their peers. Such technology is now ever present and it seems many schools have adopted a set of these tools; we do not recommend any particular suite or set of software—our interest is what you do with them as teachers and as learners.

STUDENTS NEED TO BELIEVE THAT THEIR GROUPS WILL IMPACT THEIR COLLECTIVE AND INDIVIDUAL LEARNING AND SEEK EVIDENCE OF THE IMPACT OF THEIR EFFORTS.

What collaborative routines will work given my students, my content, and the tools that I have?

_____

_____

_____

_____

_____

_____

_____

_____

_____

_____

_____

TEXT RENDERING

Sometimes the goal of the group interaction is to identify key ideas from a text. For example, this could be from a fictional text in a British literature class, a research article in clinical nursing, or a whitepaper in international finance. The **text rendering** protocol is useful in this situation and is easily adapted to distance learning. Essentially, students read the text in advance and then meet to "render" it. Here is the protocol:

1. As they read, students are asked to identify an important *sentence*, *phrase*, and *word* and place them into an online collaborative document. These have to be from different parts of the reading.

2. When they meet in the live session, they each take a turn sharing their sentence.

3. Then they take turns sharing their phrases.

4. Finally, they share their words.

5. Then they discuss what they have noticed about patterns in their selections.

The person who is farthest to the left on the video display is the person who keeps the conversation going.

How can I use text rendering in my distance learning classes?

When students meet in groups without a protocol like this, they may not know how to start and may wander from the text. In this case, the words in the collaborative document foster the conversations they have. And they know that they will be required to summarize their understanding of the text on their own when the discussion is over.

JIGSAW

In essence, **jigsaw** is an approach in which students are members of two different groups: a home group and an expert group. Each time they meet with a group, there are different purposes and tasks. Over the course of the jigsaw, students deepen their understanding of the text and have opportunities to develop and practice their communication and social skills. The effect size of jigsaw is 1.20— super powerful, when done well. There are many ways to implement the jigsaw, but it's key that students talk with others during the process. Indeed, it was not created for online learning (it was invented in the arts), but it seems built for distance and remote learning. It's not just divide-and-conquer reading in which the text is divided up and students tell each other what they read. For example, consider the following implementation of an online jigsaw.

THE EFFECT SIZE OF JIGSAW IS 1.20 – SUPER POWERFUL, WHEN DONE WELL.

The students in Lou Ann Smith's Math 107 class were reading from their digital mathematics textbook. This particular chapter focused on the different ways to solve a quadratic equation. Here's how it worked:

Step 1: In their expert groups, which they could do themselves off-line, each student had been assigned the same section of the chapter—a particular way to solve a quadratic (e.g., factoring, completing the square, quadratic formula, or graphing). They read this section, prepared to teach this particular approach, and were asked to consider several questions:

- What do you not understand or are confused about?
- What makes sense to you?
- What do you want to know more about?

They shared their responses to these topics with other members of their expert groups in a breakout room. They collaborated to ensure that each member of the group had a working knowledge of the section of the text they had been assigned.

Step 2: Each member of the group had been assigned a letter and when the timer was up, Dr. Smith regrouped students so that all of the Gs were together, all of the Js were together, all of the Ks were together, and all of the Ls were together (he selects random letters so that students don't think that they are in the A group). The students were each asked to join their unique chat room and share with the others in their new (home) group their thinking about their assigned section. They had to model and teach how to solve quadratics using factoring, completing the square, the quadratic equation, and graphing. Their peers, who had not read that section, took notes, highlighted, completed practice problems, and added digital comments to that section. They specifically talked about what made sense and what did not. The purpose was to summarize the big ideas.

Step 3: Students returned to their original expert groups or chat rooms and reported back what they learned in Step 2. They talked about how their specific approach fit within the big idea of solving quadratics. They looked for similarities and differences and other relationships between the approaches.

Step 4: In this case, Dr. Smith added another step and invited each group to report what they learned to the whole class. Dr. Smith also could have then asked them a task that used the knowledge and understanding they had derived from this first round—as at minimum all students had been exposed to the main ideas, engaged and heard content, knew subject matter vocabulary, and had been introduced to the four approaches to solving a quadratic.

Reciprocal Teaching. Another collaborative task that works in a distance learning format is reciprocal teaching (Palincsar & Brown, 1984). The effect size for reciprocal teaching is 0.74. In this routine, students are assigned a comprehension strategy: predicting, summarizing, clarifying, or questioning. Each group stops at predetermined times to share their thinking using the strategy that they have been assigned.

THE EFFECT SIZE FOR RECIPROCAL TEACHING IS 0.74.

Mandi Bradley uses reciprocal teaching in her online biology class. She shares documents with her students that include stopping points for their discussions. Dr. Bradley's students are required to video record their conversations and submit them to her on the class learning management system. Dr. Bradley uses a rubric to provide students feedback about their discussion (see Figure 7.3). As she points out,

> My students can schedule their reading and discussion any time during the week that they want. But I do want to see the video recording to provide feedback and to ensure that they are engaged in respectful conversations with each other. Some of my students do this late at night, which is fine with me. I just want to make sure that they are reading so that their background knowledge and vocabulary grows. For some students, I send the document with a voice recording so that they can hear me read it. For other students, I record an introduction so that they have more information. With distance learning, I can provide some additional scaffolds and no one else in the class needs to know.

Importantly, appropriate scaffolding has an effect size of 0.58. As Dr. Bradley notes, when teachers are able to provide a range of scaffolds, students learn more. Further, cooperative learning has an effect size of 0.40. This aspect of distance learning has the potential to accelerate students' performance when done well.

Figure 7.3	Internet Reciprocal Teaching Dialogue Rubric				
RT Strategy	**Beginning 1**	**Developing 2**	**Accomplished 3**	**Exemplary 4**	**Score**
Questioning	Generates simple recall questions that can be answered directly from factors or information found within the website's home page	Generates main idea questions that can be answered based on information gathered by accessing one or more links to the website's content	Generates questions requiring inference; facts and information must be synthesized from one or more links to the website's content and combined with prior knowledge	Generates questions flexibly that vary in type, based on the content read and the direction of the dialogue	
Clarifying	Identifies clarification as a tool to enhance understanding and initiates clarification dialogue when appropriate	Identifies appropriate words for clarification with the dialogue's context	Assists group in clarifying identified words based on context clues	Uses strategies for word clarification that can be applied generally across reading contexts	

(Continued)

(Continued)

RT Strategy	Beginning 1	Developing 2	Accomplished 3	Exemplary 4	Score
Summarizing	Summary consists of loosely related titles	Summary consists of several main ideas but also many details	Summary synthesizes main ideas, is complete, accurate, and concise	Summary is accurate, complete, and concise, incorporating content vocabulary contained in the text	
Predicting	Demonstrates knowledge of predictions as an active reading strategy	Directs group predictions to set a clear purpose for reading	Articulates predications that build logically from context	Provides justification for prediction and initiates confirmation or redirection based on information located in text	

Source: Created by Jill Castek for Teach New Literacies. Retrieved from https://teachnewliteracies.wordpress.com/internet-reciprocal-teaching/

NOTE TO SELF

How can I use jigsaw or reciprocal teaching with my students?

COACHING AND FACILITATING

Speaking of scaffolding, this aspect of distance learning is one of the primary ways that teachers can support students. Often, this is done with small groups or individuals. Essentially, this aspect of the learning focuses on guiding students' thinking while avoiding the temptation to tell them what to think. This requires that professors ask the right question to get the student to do the work and teach the students how to ask powerful questions. Questioning has an effect size of 0.48.

It is also noted, however, that PreK–12 teachers dominate the class in terms of questions, and questions are the second most dominant teaching method after teacher talk (Cotton, 2001). The estimates of questions per day vary between 100 and 350 (Brualdi, 1998; Clinton & Dawson, 2018; Levin & Long, 1981; Mohr, 1998) and the responses from the teacher questions to the students is typically some form of recall of facts, judgment, or correction, primarily reinforcing in nature, affirming, restating, and consolidating student responses. In over 80 percent of the teacher questions, they already know the answer (Shomoossi, 2004); most of the questions are closed with low cognitive demands on students (see Asay & Orgill, 2010; Erdogan & Campbell, 2008; Nystrand, Wu, Gamoran, Zeiser, & Long, 2001); and the most common form of interaction is still the IRE cycle: *initiate* a question, get a *response*, and teacher *evaluates* the response. There is no reason to believe that this is not also the case in college and university classrooms.

"Authentic questions, like uptake, also contribute to coherence. By asking authentic questions, teachers elicit students' ideas, opinions, and feelings, and in so doing, they make students' prior knowledge and values available as a context for processing new information. [Thus they] . . . contribute to the coherence of instruction by enlarging the network of available meanings in the class" (Nystrand, Gamoran, & Carbonaro, 1998, p. 19).

One of the downsides of questioning whole classes is the low participation by many students in the question answering. Randolph (2007) found that response cards were powerful in increasing participation (by 50%) and were preferred by students (82%) to hand raising. Response cards are cards, signs, or items that are simultaneously held up by all students in the class to display their responses to questions or problems. Students using response cards, on average, performed higher on quizzes (d = 1.08) and higher on tests (d = 0.38) in the response card condition than in the hand-raising condition.

We are impressed with Marty Nystrand and colleagues' (1998) notion of the "uptake" question where teachers (or students) validate particular student ideas by incorporating their responses into subsequent questions and "authentic" questions whereby questions are asked to obtain valued information, not simply to see what students know and don't know. These authentic questions are questions without "prespecified" answers, and like uptake questions, also aim to contribute to coherence.

When questions fail to ensure success, teachers can rely on prompts and cues. In general, prompts are statements made by the teacher to focus students on

THERE ARE TIMES IN WHICH PROFESSORS MEET WITH GROUPS OF STUDENTS FOR COACHING. IN THIS CASE, PROFESSORS MEET WITH A SMALL GROUP OF STUDENTS, BASED ON THEIR IDENTIFIED LEARNING NEEDS.

PLANNING

the cognitive and metacognitive processes needed to complete a learning task. Metacognitive strategies have an effect size of 0.55. When teachers provide prompts, their students apprentice into cognitive and metacognitive thinking.

For example, history professor Jason Biggs said to a group of students during their video meeting, "I'm thinking of the video we watched that showed what life was like when the Missions were being built." In this case, he provided a background knowledge prompt. Later, he said, "I'm thinking about what we don't yet fully understand and what we can do to figure things out," which is a reflective prompt focused on metacognition. Four common prompts with examples are provided in Figure 7.4.

Figure 7.4 Types of Prompts

Type of Prompt	Definition	Example
Background knowledge	Reference to content that the student already knows, has been taught, or has experienced but has temporarily forgotten or is not applying correctly	• When trying to solve a right-triangle problem, the professor says, "What do you recall about the degrees inside a triangle?" • As part of a science passage about the water cycle, the professor says, "What do you remember about energy transfer with the states of matter?"
Process or procedure	Reference to established or generally agreed-upon representation, rules, or guidelines that the student is not following due to error or misconception	• When a student incorrectly orders fractions thinking the greater the denominator, the greater the fraction, the teacher might say, "Draw a picture of each fraction. What do you notice about the size of the fraction and the number in the denominator?" • When a student was unsure about how to start solving a problem, the professor said, "Think about which of the problem solving strategies we have used that might help you get started." • When the student has difficulty starting to develop a writing outline, the professor says, "I'm thinking about the mnemonic we've used for organizing an explanatory article."
Reflective	Promotion of metacognition—getting the student to think about their thinking—so that the student can use the resulting insight to determine next steps or the solution to a problem	• The student has just produced a solution incorrectly, and the professor says, "Does that make sense? Think about the numbers you are working with and the meaning of the operation." • A professor says, "I see you're thinking strategically. What would be the next logical step?" • When the student fails to include evidence in their writing, the professor says, "What are we learning today? What was our purpose?"
Heuristic	Engagement in an informal, self-directed problem-solving procedure The approach the student comes up with does not have to be like anyone else's approach, but it does need to work	• When the student does not get the correct answer to a math problem, the professor says, "Maybe drawing a visual representation would help you see the problem." • When the student has difficulty explaining the relationships between characters in a text, the professor says, "Maybe drawing a visual representation of the main character's connections to one another will help you."

Type of Prompt	Definition	Example
		• When the student does not get the correct answer to a math problem, the professor says, "Maybe drawing a visual representation would help you see the problem." • When the student has difficulty explaining the relationships between characters in a text, the professor says, "Maybe drawing a visual representation of the main character's connections to one another will help you."

Source: Adapted from Fisher, D., & Frey, N. (2013). *Better learning through structured teaching: A framework for the gradual release of responsibility* (2nd ed.). Alexandria, VA: ASCD.

Cues, on the other hand, are designed to shift a student's attention. Sometimes, students need this level of support to work through something that is confusing. For example, AnnaMarie Franklin, a mathematics professor, was working with a group of students and they seemed to miss the exponent in the problem. She used the highlight function on the virtual whiteboard to shift her students' attention to that part of the problem and it worked. As one student said, "OMG, I totally missed that. I thought it was a mixed fraction and it's an exponent." Again, the professor does not simply tell the student what to think, but rather shifts the learner's attention to something that is likely to help. Figure 7.5 includes a list of common cues and examples.

Figure 7.5   Types of Cues

Type of Cue	Definition	Example
Visual	A range of graphic hints that guide students through thinking or understanding	• Highlighting places on a text where students have made errors • Creating a graphic organizer to arrange content visually • Asking students to take a second look at a graphic or visual from a textbook
Verbal	Variations in speech used to draw attention to something specific or verbal attention getters that focus students' thinking	• "This is important: _____." • "This is the tricky part. Be careful and be sure to _____." • Repeating a student's statement using a questioning intonation • Changing volume or speed of speech for emphasis
Gestural	Professor's body movements or motions used to draw attention to something that has been missed	• Making a hand motion that has been taught in advance such as one used to indicate the importance of summarizing or predicting while reading • Placing thumbs around a key idea in a text that the student was missing
Environmental	Using the surroundings, and things in the surroundings, to influence students' understanding	• Using algebra tiles, magnetic letters, or other manipulatives to guide students' thinking • Moving an object or person so that the orientation changes and guides thinking

Source: Adapted from Fisher, D., & Frey, N. (2014). *Better learning through structured teaching: A framework for the gradual release of responsibility* (2nd ed.). Alexandria, VA: ASCD.

In addition to lessons that rely on questions, prompts, and cues to address errors and misconceptions, there are times when teachers meet with groups of students for coaching. In this case, teachers meet with a small group of students, based on their identified learning needs, and provide instruction. For example, a group of students in English professor Michael Gayle's composition class did not provide evidence in their writing. He met with them online to provide coaching about this necessary part of the task.

In other cases, these sessions are less focused on the specific academic content that students need to learn and are more focused on social skills, communication skills, or interpersonal skills. For example, ethnic studies professor Lauren Muhonja noticed that some of her students were not reaching consensus about the ideas in the text they were reading. She took notes while watching their video and scheduled a time to meet with them. As part of the coaching session, she provided the students with a recorded example from another group (with their permission) and asked what they noticed from observing these other students.

"They listen better than we do," one student said.

A second student added, "Yeah, and they talk one at a time. Also, they were able to get the work done pretty fast. We take forever and it's not always really good when we're done."

"I like how they compromised," a third student said. "They got to a good place and they could all support it."

"What do you think you could try so that your group meetings are more productive?" Dr. Muhonja asked.

The students shared ideas and Dr. Muhonja made a list. After several minutes, she shared her screen, adding, "I think that this summarizes your ideas. Can you take a minute and review my notes so we can revise or add to it?"

NOTE TO SELF

How can I plan the prompts and cues my students may need?

The students did and their conversation continued. Over time, they reached agreement and committed to try out their new plans. They each took a picture of the screen and promised to have that open the next time they met. At the end of their meeting, Dr. Muhonja said, "I hope you are proud of yourselves and I look forward to your future conversations. These are really good skills to build; they're important in a lot of contexts."

Later, reflecting on the experience, Dr. Muhonja said, "The interesting thing about distance learning is time. Some groups need a lot more time and other need less time. In my physical classroom, everyone has to stop at the same time so that we can go on with the lesson. In distance learning, if a group takes two hours to reach consensus and develop their product, it's totally fine. The point is that they're learning."

Helina Hoyt (San Diego State University, Nursing) discusses the use of simulations in remote learning.

resources.corwin.com/DLPlaybook-college

PRACTICING

The final aspect of our instructional model focuses on practice. And students need a lot of practice. One might even suggest overpracticing if they are going to learn something and then be able to apply it. Consider reading. Yes, as young children we needed to be taught to read. But if we had never practiced it, the instruction was not likely to stick. The same is true for all of the other things that students need to learn. Can you imagine never practicing the guitar, Spanish, or baseball and yet still expect to excel at it? Not likely to happen. Students need to engage in practice as part of their distance learning experiences.

One of the findings related to practice in the Visible Learning database is that *spaced practice* is much more effective than *mass practice*. In fact, the effect size of spaced practice is 0.65. The implication for distance learning (not to mention face-to-face classes) is that students should cycle through practice experiences across time. Rather than assign fifteen odd-numbered problems on a given day, space them out. And include problems from the past so that students still have to apply their knowledge to those types of challenges. It's better to have students practice thirty minutes each day rather than 2.5 hours on Friday.

In addition, *deliberate practice* is important. The effect size is 0.79. We recognize that "practice" is often equated with "mindless repetitions," which is counter to deliberate practice. To get the effect size of 0.79, students must focus their attention and engage in the tasks with the specific goal of improving performance, and there needs to be feedback that helps students know where best to move next in their learning. Goals are important. For example, the effect size of appropriately challenging goals is 0.50. Having learning goals versus not having them has an effect size of 0.51. And committing to a goal has an effect size of 0.40. Key to this is that students have a mastery goal orientation rather than a performance goal orientation. In other words, it's more valuable to say, "I want to learn to write well" or "I want to use my writing to create changes in the world" than to say, "I want to get an A on this essay" or "I want to pass this class." When students have goals, they are more likely to engage in deliberate practice.

STUDENTS NEED A LOT OF PRACTICE. ONE MIGHT EVEN SUGGEST OVERPRACTICING IF THEY ARE GOING TO LEARN SOMETHING AND THEN BE ABLE TO APPLY IT.

PLANNING

One of the key aspects of *deliberate practice* is the development of a mental representation. A mental representation is like a really well-developed mental model of how the world should work. As Ericsson and Pool (2016) noted, mental representations are "preexisting patterns of information—facts, images, rules relationships, and so on—that are held in long-term memory and that can be used to respond quickly and effectively in certain types of situations. The thing that all mental representations have in common is that they make it possible to process large amounts of information quickly, despite the limitations of short-term memory" (pp. 65–66). If students have no idea what it means to have learned something—returning back to the idea of success criteria presented in Module 5—it will be very difficult for them to develop a mental representation and thus cannot engage in deliberate practice. In other words, practice is more effective when students know why they are doing it, have a mastery goal orientation, and understand what success looks like.

NOTE TO SELF

How can I design practice experiences for my students?

Spaced

Deliberate

CONCLUSION

Designing learning experiences for students is an important aspect of every educator's job. There are any number of strategies that might work to improve students' learning. We hope that you select ones that have some evidence that they are likely to be effective. And we hope that you will monitor your students' learning and make adjustments if they are not making progress. We presented a range of instructional routines organized into an instructional framework that includes demonstrating, coaching and facilitating, collaborating, and practicing. As a final task for this module, now that you have considered instructional design for distance learning, complete the following self-assessment.

Margaret Marangione (Blue Ridge Community College, English) explains how to develop authentic, independent tasks from a distance.

resources.corwin.com/ DLPlaybook-college

FACTOR	USING THE "TRAFFIC LIGHT" SCALE, EVALUATE YOUR CURRENT LEVEL OF IMPLEMENTATION (GREEN IS GOOD OR REGULARLY; RED IS THE OPPOSITE).	USING THE SCALE BELOW, DETERMINE HOW IMPORTANT THIS FACTOR IS FOR YOU.
Demonstrating		not at all · somewhat · very · extremely
Collaborating		not at all · somewhat · very · extremely
Coaching and facilitating		not at all · somewhat · very · extremely
Practicing		not at all · somewhat · very · extremely

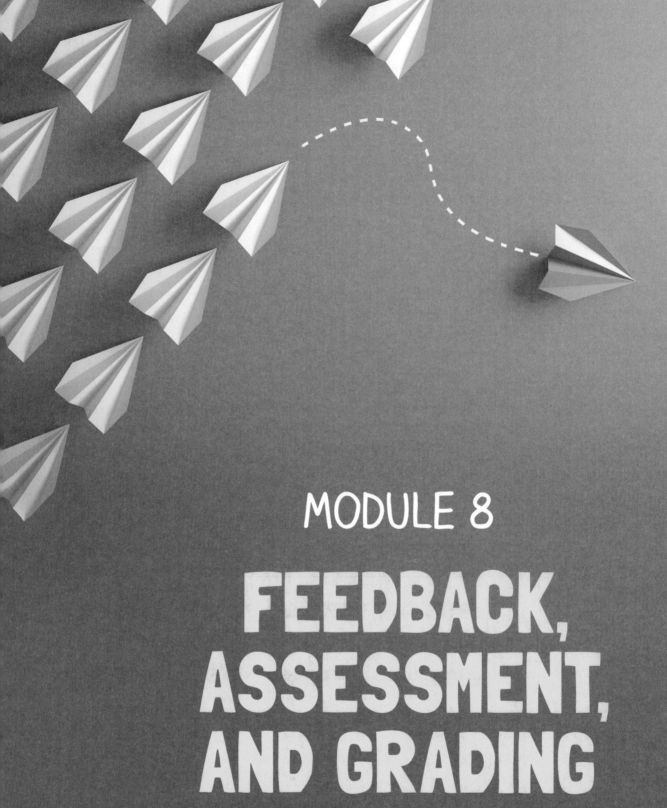

MODULE 8

FEEDBACK, ASSESSMENT, AND GRADING

The link between feedback and assessment is a strong one. Assessment drives feedback, as evidenced each time a faculty member checks for understanding and responds to what has been observed. Even better, assessments used formatively shape feedback and instruction as faculty determine what needs to be learned next in the face of what has been and what has not yet been learned. Feedback drives learning, as the student utilizes the feedback to improve performance. Grades are derived from performance on assessments that are used summatively.

Assessment is assessment. Any assessment can be used formatively or summatively. In other words, there's nothing magical in the tool itself; it's what you do with it (or don't do with teaching practices). It has the potential to be eye-opening—to help us consider what worked and what didn't as we carefully examine the evidence of student progress. Unfortunately, it has more often been used as an isolated measure of a given student's achievement at one point in time than it has as a nuanced consideration of the overall trajectory of their learning experience (e.g., a final exam in HIST 350 or BIO 360). Feedback is the connective tissue in the assessment system. It serves as a way to drive learning in the moment and when the learning is measured cumulatively. Grades give further feedback to the student as a measure of mastery.

Laura Bowman, psychology professor, describes these as "links in a paper chain." Her students at times are in a face-to-face classroom, while at other points in the semester they have been in a remote learning environment. "The learning has to continue, regardless of where it's occurring. There are some adjustments that I make depending on the setting. What I've done is shift my feedback processes so that there's more continuity in either setting."

She used the example of a recent experiment her students completed online. Dr. Bowman explained that they had been studying principles of the Stroop effect, which holds that incongruent stimuli affects response time. You've probably seen this.

Color names are written on flashcards in either the correct color font, or an incorrect one. Thus, the word "green" is sometimes written in a green font (congruent) or in a yellow font (incongruent). Her students took an online Stroop test and entered their completion times and percentage of accuracy on a collaborative document. Later the same week, students used the data to draw conclusions in a formal report.

"As I read each student's results, I recorded a short video to provide them with in-the-moment feedback," she said. "I also noticed there was a pattern to an error in building their scatterplots I was seeing. So I also recorded a new lesson for them to watch in which I revisited outliers, direction, form, and strength. Students who needed to, redid their lab report and resubmitted," she recalled. "In the past, it would have been difficult for them to get their heads wrapped around the idea of revising and resubmitting. But we've made this a core process whether we are face-to-face or in distance learning. And I'm giving them feedback and recorded lessons on our learning management system whether we're physically together or not. It makes shifting between mediums a lot simpler."

The shift to distance learning has raised questions about how feedback, assessment, and grading might be affected in virtual environments. As with previous modules, we ask you to leverage what you already know about this subject in your face-to-face classroom experiences. Take a few minutes to identify your goals for each and how you know you are achieving these goals. You'll revisit these goals at the end of the module.

DRAWING ON MY EXPERTISE

What are your goals for each? How do you assess whether you have achieved these goals?

	GOALS	EVIDENCE OF SUCCESS TOWARD GOALS
Feedback to Students	• _____ • _____ • _____ • _____ • _____ • _____ • _____ • _____ • _____	• _____ • _____ • _____ • _____ • _____ • _____ • _____ • _____ • _____

	GOALS	EVIDENCE OF SUCCESS TOWARD GOALS
Formative Evaluation	• _____ • _____ • _____ • _____ • _____ • _____ • _____ • _____ • _____	• _____ • _____ • _____ • _____ • _____ • _____ • _____ • _____ • _____
Summative Evaluation	• _____ • _____ • _____ • _____ • _____ • _____ • _____ • _____ • _____	• _____ • _____ • _____ • _____ • _____ • _____ • _____ • _____ • _____
Grading	• _____ • _____ • _____ • _____ • _____ • _____ • _____ • _____ • _____	• _____ • _____ • _____ • _____ • _____ • _____ • _____ • _____ • _____

FEEDBACK TO STUDENTS

Feedback has been described as the most underutilized instructional approach we have at our disposal. Faculty members will often say that they know feedback is useful, but they offer *useful* feedback surprisingly infrequently, with most incidents consisting of general praise of a nonspecific nature ("You've done a fantastic job!"), and usually only one or two sentences in length (Voerman, Meijer, Korthagen, & Simons, 2012). It truly is a lost opportunity as well, since the effect size of feedback is 0.66 and likely to have a positive impact on student learning (Hattie, 2018). The purpose of feedback should remain constant—to progressively close the gap between present and desired performance (Hattie & Timperley, 2007).

ASSESSMENTS USED FORMATIVELY SHAPE FEEDBACK AND INSTRUCTION.

But the usefulness of feedback varies considerably. Corrective feedback alone isn't especially effective for anything other than new learning. For example, corrective feedback during a problem-solving session with Calculus I students who are just learning about integration by parts is useful ("No, that's not correct, the answer is . . ."). But much of the feedback provided to students concerns their application of knowledge. Telling a student, "Your answer to this word problem is wrong—the answer is 24" is less effective, because it doesn't provide any additional information about the processes they used or the path forward. What exactly do they need to work on to arrive at an answer of 24? There is not enough information in this feedback to close the gap between present and desired performance.

More effective is the use of high-information feedback that consists of corrective feedback coupled with information about processes and self-regulation (Wisniewski, Zierer, & Hattie, 2020). These dense feedback units address the three major questions learners have:

- Where am I going?
- How am I going there?
- Where will I go next?

Bobby Chambers (San Diego City College, Communications) discusses the importance of giving and receiving feedback.

resources.corwin.com/ DLPlaybook-college

WHERE AM I GOING?

The first question is addressed through the learning intentions and success criteria. Knowing what success looks like allows students to work toward their learning goals. Feedback can be used to ensure students information about their approximation of the learning. For example, English professor Smita Agarwal recorded voice feedback on a student's online draft essay comparing Orson Welles's *Citizen Kane* and Coleridge's poem "Kubla Khan." She began by saying, "You provided an overview of each text, citing relevant details from both. This sets the context of your comparison for the reader. What's missing so far is a clear focus on your lines of comparison. Across what aspects are you comparing these two texts?"

HOW AM I GOING THERE?

The second question concerns the use of strategies that might address the discrepancies between execution and success. Dr. Agarwal added, "So let's talk for a few minutes about where you might locate this information. Developing a Venn diagram or some other graphic organizer for comparing and contrasting is going to help you organize your thinking and essay."

WHERE WILL I GO NEXT?

The third question is answered when we shift the focus to the student's future actions. Dr. Agarwal continued, "What's next for you? It's important that you have a plan. What are two or three things you're going to do?" Feedback, as Brookhart (2008) describes it, needs to be "just-in-time, just-for-me information delivered when and where it can do the most good" (p. 1).

THE SOCIOEMOTIONAL LINKS TO FEEDBACK

When students are engaged in appropriately challenging tasks, they are more likely to respond to feedback because they need that information to continue growing and learning. Feedback focused on something that you already know does little to change understanding. And feedback thrives on errors. When errors are celebrated and expected, feedback can gain a foothold. The relationship between the person providing the feedback and the person receiving it has a mediating effect on the usefulness of the feedback. But it's only when the feedback is received that it works. Consider the complex dimensions that are required to accomplish this:

- The relationship between the faculty member and student needs to be a positive one.

- Faculty need to be seen as credible in the eyes of the student.

- The climate of the class needs to be such that errors are not viewed with shame, but as part of the learning process.

In the PreK–12 environment, the receiving of feedback is correlated with the student–teacher relationship. For example, in a study of middle and high school students' attitudes about feedback on their writing, Zumbrunn and her colleagues (2016) found that 20 percent of them disregarded it because they didn't have a good relationship with their teachers. While the study didn't explore the nature of these relationships between college and university faculty and their students, it seems apparent that feedback requires effort on the part of the teacher. It is discouraging to think that one out of five students might potentially reject our feedback out of hand.

CORRECTIVE FEEDBACK ALONE ISN'T ESPECIALLY EFFECTIVE FOR ANYTHING OTHER THAN NEW LEARNING.

NOTE TO SELF

Select a well-designed student task you have used before (see Module 6 for a refresher on engaging tasks). What do you need to do to provide high-information feedback?

"Where am I going?"

Success Criteria

"How am I going there?"

Feedback About Processes

"Where will I go next?"

Self-Regulatory Feedback

Something we wonder about is whether in some cases the feedback is misplaced. It doesn't work across the board for all situations. In fact, in their meta-analyses on feedback, Wisniewski, Zierer, and Hattie (2020) report that "feedback has higher impact on cognitive and motor skills outcomes than on motivational and behavioral outcomes" (p. 1). Yet how often is feedback used in a misguided attempt to motivate or change behavior? Confine your feedback to the more effective realms of cognitive and motor skills, while remaining cognizant of the social and emotional conditions required to make your feedback useful.

NOTE TO SELF

In what ways do you foster social and emotional elements of learning to leverage feedback? What errors do you want to avoid?

	WAYS YOU FOSTER	ERRORS TO AVOID
Teacher–Student Relationships		
Teacher Credibility		
Classroom Climate That Accepts Errors		

FEEDBACK AT A DISTANCE

Technology offers great possibilities when it comes to distance learning. The highest effects of digital technology are interactive videos (0.54) and intelligent tutoring systems (0.51).

Interactive videos, whether faculty generated or commercially produced, require students to respond to questions interspersed throughout. Practices like this are commonly done in face-to-face teaching, such as using interactive problem-solving sessions that are punctuated with questions about the practices and processes utilized to solve the problems. However, interactive videos offer a superior advantage that can't be fully replicated in live teaching: The student can view it again and again. This reduces the cognitive overload students might otherwise experience because they can rewatch segments that are more difficult. In addition, interactive videos are associated with increased attention and greater reflection, likely due to increased student choice and control. As one example, you can rewatch the video of Stuart Voytilla as he describes formative assessments and checks for understanding. This video not only talks about formative assessments, but how to utilize these checks for understanding with learners through interactive videos.

Intelligent tutoring systems (ITS) are commercially produced and mirror many of the best features of feedback. Information is presented and the system asks questions, provides feedback or hints, and gives prompts. Based on the student's responses, the system adapts questions, feedback, and prompts (Ma, Adesope, Nesbit, & Liu, 2014). Examples of ITS programs include AutoTutor, Cognitive Tutor, and ALEKS. It should be noted that ITS programs are not "plug and play" and require investment in professional learning for teachers.

Easier to implement are feedback mechanisms that capitalize on your knowledge of the students and your relationship with them. The Read&Write function on Google Docs allows you to highlight a portion of a student's submitted work and record a voice comment for feedback. As noted in Module 3, voice-recorded comments give you the opportunity to use students' names and give them the chance to hear the warmth and tone behind the feedback. Unlike a written comment, which is a bit more decontextualized, a recorded comment comes closer to simulating the kind of verbal feedback you would offer in a face-to-face setting. These voice notes offer another important opportunity, as students can also record questions and comments for the teacher.

Feedback from the student to the teacher is especially important in distance learning. Be sure to

- Solicit feedback from students regularly to find out how they are experiencing their online learning.

- Ask them about the videos and materials you have been preparing for them and whether they find them useful, or whether they are using them at all.

THE RELATIONSHIP BETWEEN THE PERSON PROVIDING THE FEEDBACK AND THE PERSON RECEIVING IT HAS A MEDIATING EFFECT ON THE USEFULNESS OF THE FEEDBACK. BUT IT'S ONLY WHEN THE FEEDBACK IS RECEIVED THAT IT WORKS.

- Find out about their own self-regulation by asking them to reflect on the previous week and note whether they asked a question of the teacher outside of the live session.

Couple this with the user analytics you can gather on how often various materials and videos were accessed on your learning management system (LMS) to gather data in real time. The feedback gained from students gives you direction about what to continue, what to do more of, and what isn't especially useful to them.

NOTE TO SELF

What special considerations do you need to keep in mind when providing feedback to students in a virtual environment? How will you solicit feedback from students?

FORMATIVE EVALUATION

Dylan Wiliam makes a crucial point when he says, as David Ausubel noted more than 50 years ago, "good teaching starts from where the learner is, rather than where we would like her or him to be" (Wiliam, 2020). The practice of formative evaluation requires that we check for understanding throughout our classes, not only at the end. The practice of formative evaluation with students has been shown to be of benefit to teachers in making decisions about next steps in teaching, as measured by gains in student learning. With an effect size of 0.34, it is likely to have a positive impact on student learning. However, the power of formative evaluation doesn't reside solely in the act of administering the quiz or assignment. It is the feedback from the assessment, not the assessment itself, that matters. Its power is amplified when (1) the student and the faculty member understand the results and (2) the faculty member and the student use the results to take action on future teaching and learning. In other words, formative evaluation shouldn't be done only so we can make decisions (that's important) but also so the student can make decisions.

There are a number of ways to check for understanding, such as exit slips, story retellings, poll responses to questions, and practice quizzes. A virtual environment allows for all of these to occur, albeit in ways that may differ from methods used in a face-to-face classroom.

Stuart Voytilla (San Diego State University, TV and Film) discusses formative assessments in remote learning.

resources.corwin.com/ DLPlaybook-college

VIRTUAL EXIT SLIPS

Provide students with a range of possible responses and ask them to use the options at the end of assignments or virtual class sessions. Maria Cordova, finance professor, asks her students to gauge their level of understanding at the end of each class meeting. Her students are given four possible responses to choose from:

1. I'm just learning (I need more help).

2. I'm almost there (I need more practice).

3. I own it (I can work independently).

4. I'm a veteran CPA (I can teach others).

Dr. Cordova said, "I get their feedback about where they think they are in their first course in tax accounting, and that helps me plan for some specialized support for the next class meeting. This is their first real experience with federal tax accounting, and I need to make sure they are with me. Once a week, I schedule a live session and divide them up based on their feedback. I manually populate breakout rooms with those students who have ranked themselves as a 2 or a 3 so they can support one another." Those students who feel like they can teach others are generally smaller in number, "so I distribute them carefully in breakout rooms that might need some additional expertise with tax returns." She chooses tasks for these breakout rooms that are culled from the week's assignments that proved to be more challenging. "So, I give them ten minutes or so to work through a parallel tax return together."

In the meantime, Dr. Cordova is meeting up with a small group of students who had asked for more help. "It's a chance for me to reteach and find out where their barriers lie. If I need more time with individual students, I schedule an additional session just for them to meet during virtual office hours." She calls this portion of her online class Mastery Monday so that her students always know when to expect this routine. "The whole thing only takes about fifteen minutes, but it is a great warm-up for all of us. When we return to the main room, it becomes our first whole-class discussion. I ask them, "What are you learning about yourself as a learner? As a future accountant?" because I want to reinforce the value in persistence and collaborative problem solving in business finance."

John Almarode (James Madison University, Education) explains how to generate student self-feedback and peer-to-peer feedback.

resources.corwin.com/DLPlaybook-college

VIRTUAL RETELLINGS

Retellings are most commonly used with elementary students for a variety of purposes, including fostering listening comprehension, oral composition, sequencing ability, attention, and memory. For younger children, retellings allow teachers to determine whether a child can process language when the burden of reading a text is removed. One of the easiest ways to do this is to read a short text to a student and then invite them to retell the story. However, we can adjust this strategy for our students as well.

Vincent Romero, professor of public policy and administration, uses virtual retellings in his Politics of International Relations course. "In this specific area, comprehension, oral composition, and attention are very important. I ask my students to read a policy document and listen to a recording of an 'ambassador' discussing the policy document." Dr. Romero posts this on the course LMS so that students can listen to the discussion multiple times. "I can see how many times students listen to the recording." Each week, Dr. Romero selects three or four students to record a summarization of the policy. Then, "the other students use a rubric focused on the precision, accuracy, and clarity of their summarization. How well did they use clear and concise language to communicate the policy? If they plan to have a career in international relations, communication is key."

VOICE-RECORDED COMMENTS GIVE YOU THE OPPORTUNITY TO USE STUDENTS' NAMES AND GIVE THEM THE CHANCE TO HEAR THE WARMTH AND TONE BEHIND THE FEEDBACK.

POLLING TO RESPOND TO QUESTIONS

Faculty have increasingly used polls to solicit information from students in face-to-face environments, and they prove to be even more useful in distance learning environments. As one example, Maria Cardillo, professor of foreign languages

(Italian), regularly includes Kahoot! questions (a game-based learning platform) about Italian literature and culture as a way to check for understanding and a way for her students to get immediate feedback. Students respond on their cell phones to multiple choice questions, and a bar graph populates on the shared screen to gauge the number of correct and incorrect responses. Similar polling functions are often built in to learning management systems and provide feedback to both faculty and students in real time about the current status of the learning.

PRACTICE TESTS

Formative practice testing, in which students take short quizzes to understand their command of the subject or topic, is an effective way to check for understanding while also prompting deliberative practice. These formative practice tests are low stakes and not part of the student's grade, as the emphasis here is on practice to gain self-knowledge of learning gaps. A meta-analysis of the effectiveness of formative practice testing on advancing student learning reported these findings (Adesope, Trevisan, & Sundararajan, 2017):

- Lots of practice tests didn't increase student learning. Once is often enough.

- Feedback paired with the practice test enhances learning.

- Their usefulness was strong at both the elementary and secondary levels.

- The value of formative practice tests is in students reflecting on their results.

Susan Michaels, nursing professor, uses short practice tests with her students asynchronously, then scores them and uses the results to drive a subsequent live virtual session around competencies addressed in both the nursing program and for licensure. Her students have been learning about adverse side-effects of certain drugs and how to treat this issue. Dr. Michaels previously posed questions for her students to respond to, so that she and they could gauge their understanding of the topic. After taking a five-question audience response quiz at the midpoint in the week, the students in her class analyzed their results and then met in breakout rooms aligned to the questions. "I join each group for a few minutes so I can listen in on conversations. They've gotten very used to me popping in and out."

One of her students, Olivia, did not answer two of the questions correctly but was especially puzzled by the fourth question, which asked about vasodilators and blood pressure. Olivia chose to meet with a group of students who had selected the same question so that they could build on each other's knowledge. Olivia and several other students did a search of their pharmacology textbook and

"GOOD TEACHING STARTS FROM WHERE THE LEARNER IS, RATHER THAN WHERE WE WOULD LIKE HER OR HIM TO BE."

Katie Hughes (San Diego State University, English) highlights the role of feedback in teaching writing.

resources.corwin.com/ DLPlaybook-college

reread the background information on the fluid mechanics of the blood vessels. "Oh, I remember this now!" she said. Luke, another member of the group, replayed the blood pressure interactive video lab they had completed in the previous week. "The blood vessel is dilated, and when the patient is dehydrated at the same time, a significant drop in blood pressure occurs. Let me draw it out." Olivia pointed out that, "when I watched that lab that went right past me. The drawing helped me make that connection. I like the practice quizzes Dr. Michaels gives because it helps me see things I didn't notice the first time. It gives me an idea about where my practice needs to be to prepare for the final exam in December." This example helps highlight that via distance learning students often have the chance to replay lecture videos many times, an opportunity often denied in the face-to-face classroom.

NOTE TO SELF

How do you check for understanding in your distance learning classes? Below, add other methods you are using or intend to use to check for understanding formatively and summatively.

	USEFUL AND CURRENTLY USING IT	USEFUL AND HAVEN'T USED IT YET	NOT USEFUL FOR MY CLASS
Virtual Exit Slips			
Virtual Retellings			
Polling and Audience Response Methods			
Practice Tests			

SUMMATIVE EVALUATIONS

Summative evaluations typically come at the end of a chunk or segment of instruction. In a semester course, summative evaluations may occur at the end of particular set of topics. For example, many of our colleagues break the semester into thirds, with a summative assessment coming after each third—the last third's summative evaluation being the final exam. Such assessments test cumulative knowledge and skills learned at the end of a unit of work, over a semester, or at the end of a course. The designs of these vary widely depending on students' developmental needs and the nature of the topic or course. A distance learning environment prompts additional concerns about testing security, given that a teacher's usual ability to proctor an exam in a face-to-face classroom is limited when it must be completed virtually. Having acknowledged that, here are some considerations for promoting authenticity in summative evaluations.

FORMATIVE EVALUATION SHOULDN'T BE DONE ONLY SO THE PROFESSOR CAN MAKE DECISIONS (THAT'S IMPORTANT) BUT ALSO SO THE STUDENT CAN MAKE DECISIONS.

- **Become acquainted with your LMS assessment tools.** Your learning platform likely includes features that allow for a specific timed-testing window, as well as a randomization feature that allows items to appear in a unique order for each student.

- **Proctor shorter exams in live sessions.** Use a timed live session and have students turn their cameras on so that you can observe them during the test.

- **Use text-matching software for essays.** Many colleges and universities use plagiarism detection programs as part of their online learning. Even in face-to-face settings, these are valuable teaching tools. That is key—teach students about the use of text-matching tools and don't misuse them as a way to catch them doing something wrong.

- **Expand your repertoire of assessment formats.** Oral tests have long been viewed as a useful option for some students, but the amount of time we have in face-to-face classrooms has limited their use to a smaller number of students. But in a distance learning classroom, students can record themselves presenting their summaries of their learning for the teacher to view individually.

- **Teach students about academic honesty and ethical decision making.** Take a proactive approach by embedding these topics into classroom discourse. A statement of academic honesty should be introduced in the first week of class and featured prominently on your LMS and at the beginning of each assessment. Most of all, infuse discussions about ethical decision making—a key socioemotional learning skill—into your content area when testing is not a primary focus.

This is not an exhaustive list of ways to check for understanding through summative evaluation. On the next page, we invite you to consider approaches we have highlighted and to add your own to your menu of options for checking for understanding.

CHECKING FOR UNDERSTANDING APPROACHES

What tools does my LMS offer?	
How can I proctor assessments?	
What text-matching systems can I use?	
What assessment formats can I use?	
What do I need to teach students in relation to academic honesty and ethical decision making in distance learning?	

COMPETENCY-BASED GRADING

Angie Hackman (Cuyamaca Community College, Biology) talks about competency-based assessments.

resources.corwin.com/ DLPlaybook-college

THE VALUE OF FORMATIVE PRACTICE TESTS IS IN STUDENTS REFLECTING ON THEIR RESULTS.

Most teachers will tell you that grades are given to reflect a student's mastery of a concept or subject, but upon looking deeper, you discover that several other nonacademic factors are in the formula. Let's take a fictional student and call him Javier. Did he bring materials to class? Check. Did he turn in his homework? Sometimes. Did he behave reasonably well in class? Nope. So what's his grade for the course? Naturally, you would say that this isn't enough information and you need to know what his summative evaluations looked like. Yet too often organization, compliance, and behavior are lumped in with evaluations of learning. This is not to say that these nonacademic indicators are unimportant, but rather that when factored in with learning performance they obscure the signal. And in this model, things quickly turn personal and undermine the relationship between the teacher and the learner. Instead of being able to tie his academic performance to his grade in Western Civilizations, Javier grumbles, "My professor doesn't like me. He's always on my case. That's why I'm failing." The resentment builds, Javier only gets more sullen, and now his professor really doesn't like him. Javier's learning trajectory looks increasingly dismal, and in the meantime, he continues to externalize as he blames others.

In an effort to end negative and ultimately futile cycles like this, more colleges and universities are turning to competency-based grading systems across face-to-face and distance learning settings. This system focuses on mastery of content and eliminates grading of practice work and nonacademic behaviors. For certain disciplines, competency-based grading has been in place for a long time. Areas in workforce development cannot assess their learners using multiple-choice exams or essay tests. Automation engineering, culinary arts, certified nursing assistants, and welding technology, to name a few, require that students demonstrate mastery of a particular set of skills, practices, and process. Again, a multiple-choice assessment just won't work. In this cases, students receive grades based on their performance on summative evaluations only, typically between four and six per semester. Assignments and homework are regarded as formative evaluation for both the faculty member and the student, and do not earn points toward the course grade. Of course, some students don't do the homework. However, in time most learn the value of the practice that allows them to master the content.

Because the distance learning week looks different than in a brick-and-mortar school, units of instruction are often organized as online modules that combine synchronous and asynchronous learning experiences. Students are encountering more self-paced and self-directed learning, and faculty are finding themselves relying less on in-class assignments and other small tasks. Competency-based grading has the added benefit of avoiding the error of averaging multiple tasks. Imagine if the written and performance portions of a driving test were averaged such that a failing score on one but an exemplary score on the other would result in a driver's license. Few of us would be in favor of sharing the road with someone who had either failed at operating the vehicle properly or was not knowledgeable about traffic laws.

Students in the competency-based grading model are often required to pass each summative evaluation (usually a complex performance task) at a level of 70 percent or higher. Students who do not meet this threshold receive an Incomplete, signaling to them that mastery has not yet been attained. These learners are required to attend virtual tutorials and must participate in additional practice opportunities before taking another version of the exam. Using competency-based grading has the potential to produce the following outcomes:

- With time, most students learn the value of their active participation in their learning.

- Relationships between faculty and students are healthier because much of the subjective nature of grading has been removed.

- It's really hard to implement and requires revisiting these policies regularly to revise and improve them.

TOO OFTEN ORGANIZATION, COMPLIANCE, AND BEHAVIOR ARE LUMPED IN WITH EVALUATIONS OF LEARNING.

Let's revisit the above-mentioned incomplete grade. Rather than require learners to re-take a course we can focus on what has yet to be completed. After all, it's the Incompletes that must be addressed. Therefore, some learners may take four days, while other students need a longer amount of time to meet the competencies. By no means do we suggest that in practice a competency-based grading system is clean and easy. It's messy and hard. But we hope that our students gain a deeper understanding of themselves as learners and what they need to do next to be successful. These dispositions are becoming even more crucial when students are in a distance learning environment.

You may or may not be ready to think about competency-based grading at this time. But we do hope that grading is a part of your discussions with colleagues, even if the decision is to hold steady with your current grading system. Effective departments and programs in our colleges and universities are willing to revisit procedures and policies in order to promote learning. Your willingness to have the discussion is evidence of the first mindframe: "I focus on learning and the language of learning."

NOTE TO SELF

Use these questions to spark discussion about grading practices in the context of distance learning.

What is working well for us as it pertains to grading in distance learning?

What problems are we encountering in using our current grading system in a distance learning environment?

What successful distance learning grading practices are we aware of?

How might we investigate other successful distance learning grading practices?

CONCLUSION

Formative and summative evaluation play an essential role in signaling learning progress to students, especially when they are actively engaged in viewing data, making strategic decisions, and taking action on next steps. These evaluative processes bracket the high-information feedback provided to students. These practices are even more important in a distance learning environment. Take a few minutes to revisit the goals you identified for feedback, formative evaluation, summative evaluation, and grading. Then assess yourself on the factors discussed in this module.

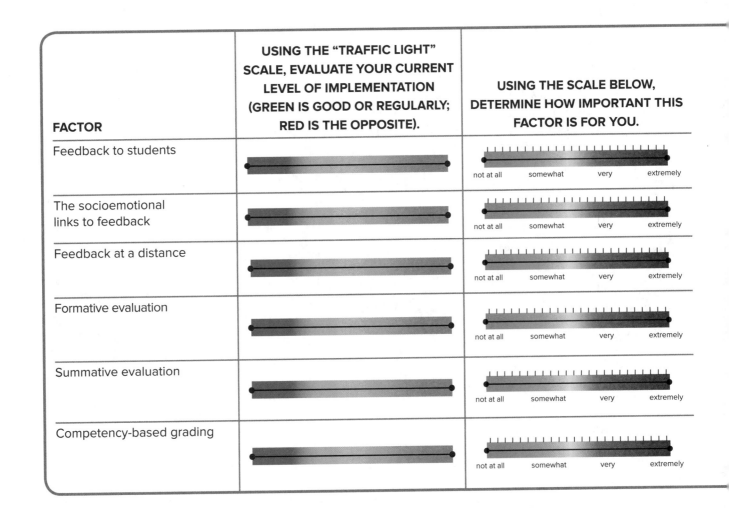

FACTOR	USING THE "TRAFFIC LIGHT" SCALE, EVALUATE YOUR CURRENT LEVEL OF IMPLEMENTATION (GREEN IS GOOD OR REGULARLY; RED IS THE OPPOSITE).	USING THE SCALE BELOW, DETERMINE HOW IMPORTANT THIS FACTOR IS FOR YOU.
Feedback to students		not at all somewhat very extremely
The socioemotional links to feedback		not at all somewhat very extremely
Feedback at a distance		not at all somewhat very extremely
Formative evaluation		not at all somewhat very extremely
Summative evaluation		not at all somewhat very extremely
Competency-based grading		not at all somewhat very extremely

KEEPING THE FOCUS ON LEARNING, DISTANCE OR OTHERWISE

Teaching and learning underwent radical change worldwide in the spring of 2020. Due to a global pandemic, learners of all ages suddenly found themselves attempting to navigate unfamiliar technologies in settings that had not previously been used as dedicated learning spaces (bedrooms, kitchen tables, and garages, to name a few). College and university faculty shifted instruction from face-to-face classrooms to virtual ones seemingly overnight. Departments and programs mobilized to get technology and WiFi access into the hands of all students who needed it. We had to learn to work from home in a way we had never done before now. In the past, we would work from home to devote uninterrupted time to writing projects or grading. Now, we had to learn to teach from home while juggling all of the additional challenges of managing children, pets, and partners. We were not longer working from home, alone. These emergency efforts focused primarily on converting what had been occurring in our classrooms, laboratories, and offices to digital spaces that were physically in the same location. We found ourselves simply clicking from one digital space to another without ever leaving our chairs. There was no time to plan for this conversion. We were in crisis mode. During that time, we learned some important lessons:

- Social and emotional elements of learning are interwoven with academic ones. We found ourselves confronted with all aspects of learning: academic, social, and emotional. We could no longer view our classes as purely academic exercises.

- Partnerships with different entities across our campuses are central, not peripheral, to education (for teachers and students). We had to collaborate and partner with student services, dining services, facilities management, local food banks and pantries, departments of health or social services, and state agencies for education. We could no longer view our academic disciplines as one of many stand-alone entities in our colleges and universities.

- Ineffective approaches to learning are ineffective in digital spaces, too. We learned that success in the new normal required that we leverage only the most effective pedagogies to ensure that our students received the highest quality of learning.

Stephanie Holmsten (University of Texas at Austin, International Relations and Global Studies) explains the importance of socioemotional learning in higher education.

resources.corwin.com/ DLPlaybook-college

While the scale of this rapid move to online learning was unprecedented, the fact that colleges and universities were able to do so is not. We have seen this before. Ask any educator who has taught in the immediate aftermath of Hurricane Katrina in New Orleans, the Christchurch earthquake in New Zealand, or the bush fires in Australia. You'll find dedicated educators who brought stability and optimism to the communities they serve, even as they dealt with their own devastation.

Here's what didn't happen: We didn't take advantage as a field to truly learn from these efforts about what to do *better*. The focus was on a return to normalcy, to the status quo. The moment we were able to, we turned our attention back to the familiar. There was no looking back to identify lessons learned and act upon them. Let's not do that this time. Instead, our focus should be on how to leverage what we are learning to make teaching and learning in our academic halls better in face-to-face and distance learning spaces. As Sir Winston Churchill is purported to have said, "Never let a crisis go to waste." There's been a crisis. How can we make sure it doesn't go to waste?

DRAWING ON MY EXPERTISE

What did you learn from crisis teaching? What will be useful in the future?

LEARNING FROM OTHER CRISES

We know from the aftermath of Hurricane Katrina in New Orleans how important it is for educators to be visible, decisive, trustworthy, respected, and willing to engage in frontline work (Porche, 2009). After Katrina, those who had a prior history of problems were more likely to show symptoms of traumatic stress, depression, sadness, anger, anxiety, and loneliness—for both students and teachers (Osofsky, Osofsky, & Harris, 2007). But the effect on PreK–12 student achievement was not as great as many expected. Students were out of school between three and seven weeks and many had no school work in this time. There was a drop of −0.17 from Katrina, but "what is more surprising is how quickly the Parish evacuees recovered from the experience and actually began to see gains in test scores" (Sacerdote, 2012, p. 131; see also Pane, McCaffrey, Kalra, & Zhou, 2008, who showed a drop of only 0.06 in statewide test scores from the outage).

An example of this resilience at the postsecondary level is Tulane University. In Tulane's history, they have closed twice. They closed for four years during the Civil War and four months after Hurricane Katrina. In the aftermath of Hurricane Katrina, they quickly leveraged partnerships with other institutions of higher learning to provide continuity in their learning.

Let's recall the effects of the Christchurch earthquakes in 2011, which severely disrupted access to schools. There was a rush to online learning with a cry for special dispensations for upper high school examinations. As advisor to the Qualifications Authority that oversaw these exams, John argued that there should not be special dispensation. He based this on strike research, which showed no effects at the upper-school level, with positive effects in some cases. Sure enough, the performance of Christchurch students went up, and as schools resumed, the scores settled back down. Why? Because, during that crisis time, teachers tailored learning more to what students could NOT do, whereas often conventional school is about what teachers *think* students need, even if students can already do the tasks. During the crisis, there was more focus on triaging learning for students and the teaching commenced from some excellent diagnoses of what students could and could not do.

The University of Canterbury responded in much the same way and then devoted time and effort to world-leading research on earthquake resilience. They have an entire research center dedicated to understanding earthquake resilience, natural and geological hazards, and hazard and disaster management. The crisis provided the impetus to learning.

In the aftermath of a crisis, students look for support from a trusted adult, seek help from peers, seek ways to express their feelings, and establish some sense of routine. Many of us, adults and children, go through feelings of shock and disorganization. There will be altruistic or heroic phases and claims, and honeymoon periods of high morale and action and optimism, but some will feel angry, displaced, and lonely.

AS SIR WINSTON CHURCHILL IS PURPORTED TO HAVE SAID, "NEVER LET A CRISIS GO TO WASTE." THERE'S BEEN A CRISIS. HOW CAN WE MAKE SURE IT DOESN'T GO TO WASTE?

Rob Gordon is an Australian who has studied the effects on schools from bushfires and talks about the desired state of social fusion: "In this state of fusion, members identify with each other because they share the same experience; they feel strong emotional attachments because of what they have undergone together and rapidly develop a shared culture of stories, symbols, and memories" (2004). Make sure every student experiences this fusion and becomes an insider in your online classroom. That colleges, universities, and classrooms already existed helps develop this bond, but now work to maintain it. Build on symbols, rituals, and identity; model connectedness; use stories and other artifacts so that when our academic buildings, research laboratories, and classrooms reopen there is a symbol, a thing, an event—a mosaic, a play, stories, collective memories of the at-home socially distancing experience.

USE CRISIS LEARNING TO MAKE COLLEGES AND UNIVERSITIES BETTER

WHAT MATTERS IS WHAT YOU DO, NOT WHERE YOU TEACH.

Technologies have allowed us to maintain learning even when brick-and-mortar classrooms and laboratories can't be used. They are increasingly instrumental to instruction in the classroom, albeit in two primary ways. The first is in presenting information. Rather than film strips, we can easily access professionally produced videos! This also shows up as narrated slide decks. The second common use of technology in the classroom is for completing independent work. Instead of boring worksheets, we can put them on a laptop and have students complete them online. If those have been the predominant digital learning experiences for students and their professors, it's little wonder that the initial shift to online learning was bumpy.

You are now likely working in two mediums: distance learning and face-to-face. What matters is what you do, not where you teach. Too much lecture and too many worksheets that are not tailored to students' needs but, rather, what we "think they need" is not effective in either environment. You may have had different experiences with using technologies in face-to-face classroom settings. We invite you to reflect on your experiences with using virtual spaces within your brick-and-mortar classroom. Some examples might include written and video discussion boards, flipped learning, online modules, student-generated collaborative documents, gamified learning, and microlearning. How often do you use them, and how do you gauge student success in these mediums?

MAKE LEARNING BETTER FOR STUDENTS

Let's remember to leverage what we have learned from crisis online learning to prepare ourselves and our students for more robust and authentic future learning.

- Focus on what students **know** and **don't know**. Only teach the things that they don't know. This was one of the most important lessons learned from the Christchurch earthquakes in New Zealand and one that should have impacted practice since then.

- Keep in mind that **there is a balance not only for students but also for teachers**. Deliver mini-classes using social media, make them clear, and provide oodles of opportunities for feedback. Make it skill based and provide exciting ways to practice, and not just project based, which can (but does not need to) lead to busy work with little learning.

- **Harness the most exciting use of technology for our current situation**. Social media has the power to enhance learning. Maree Davies and her colleagues (2017) have explored asking students to use social media on learning management systems to have students send in questions and talk about what they do not know. They are more likely to do this on social media than directly to the teacher.

- Remember, **if students get stuck, do not know what to do next, or make errors, you should not depend on roommates and family members to know about the errors or what best to do next**. We do not want roommates and family members giving feedback in a way that ends up with them doing the work!

- Take ownership as much as possible by building in mechanisms that allow for responsive ways to **provide timely feedback**.

- **Create as many opportunities for social interaction**, not just between you and the student, but using technology for students to work, share, interact, and learn together, as you often do in the regular classroom. Learning at home need not be a lonely activity, with the only or even primary resource the other members of the household.

MAKE LEARNING BETTER FOR TEACHERS

As a field, we must also look after each other during this time and in the future. Part of looking after each other is in making sure that we continue to grow professionally. Teaching is an identity and an action, not just a vocation. That leaves questions whose answers will continue to evolve. How can we

- assess our impact from a distance?

- learn how we as groups of faculty can evaluate, discuss, and work together?

- discover ways to enhance the collective efficacy of all?

- view this pandemic as an opportunity to learn more about how to work with students from afar, outside of our normal comfort zones of the academic halls and classrooms?

Annaleah Gonzalez (Cuyamaca Community College, Health Sciences) describes how to foster collective learning in higher education.

resources.corwin.com/ DLPlaybook-college

David Daniel (James Madison University, Psychology) closes with a call to focus on what matters most.

resources.corwin.com/ DLPlaybook-college

LET'S LEVERAGE WHAT WE HAVE LEARNED FROM CRISIS ONLINE LEARNING TO PREPARE FOR MORE ROBUST AND AUTHENTIC FUTURE LEARNING.

- engage with community members to realize we as educators have unique skills and expertise (and are happy to share them), and not get upset if students are not spending five or six hours every day in the belief that learning at a distance is but a mirror of the typical college learning environment?

Our colleges and universities, no matter via what medium, can be a hub of response and recovery, a place to support emotional recovery and promote social togetherness—and this is as important as any achievement gains. It would be wonderful to use this pandemic as an opportunity to learn about learning from afar, so share stories of success of colleagues and students learning from this crisis, pay particular attention to at-risk students or students with special needs, discover how to develop collective efficacy among faculty colleagues, and use this experience to learn how to best work with all students.

CONCLUSION

The implications from Visible Learning suggest that we can plan meaningful distance learning and positively impact students. Again, that's what this book is about. As you have seen from the modules in this playbook, there is evidence about what works, and we can use that evidence to ensure that our distance learning efforts mobilize what works in face-to-face and virtual environments. We invite you to engage in a final self-assessment about your learning.

FACTOR	USING THE "TRAFFIC LIGHT" SCALE, EVALUATE YOUR CURRENT LEVEL OF IMPLEMENTATION (GREEN IS GOOD OR REGULARLY; RED IS THE OPPOSITE).	USING THE SCALE BELOW, DETERMINE HOW IMPORTANT THIS FACTOR IS FOR YOU.
Learning from this crisis		not at all somewhat very extremely
Making distance learning better for students		not at all somewhat very extremely
Making distance learning better for teachers		not at all somewhat very extremely

APPENDIX

PLANNING TEMPLATE

COURSE:	INSTRUCTIONAL UNIT:			TIME RANGE:	

COMPETENCIES	TOPIC (LEARNING PROGRESSIONS)	WEEK	IN-CLASS ACTIVITIES	FORMATIVE ASSESSMENT EXTEND – REVIEW – ASSESS – RETEACH	TEXTS AND RESOURCES
		1			
		2			
		3			

Week 4: Summative Assessment Competency

Content and Academic Vocabulary

Accommodations and Modifications for Students With Special Needs

DISTANCE LEARNING LOG

STUDENT NAME:	TOPIC:
WEEK OF: (DATE)	

THIS WEEK'S LEARNING INTENTION(S)	TASKS/ASSESSMENTS I COMPLETED

SUCCESS CRITERIA

Use the space below to rate your learning before and after each class meeting.

CRITERIA	BEFORE	AFTER
I can		
I can		

online resources ↖ Available for download at **resources.corwin.com/DLPlaybook-college**

REFERENCES

Adesope, O. O., Trevisan, D. A., & Sundararajan, N. (2017). Rethinking the use of tests: A meta-analysis of practice testing. *Review of Educational Research, 87*(3), 659–701.

Alter, P., & Haydon, T. (2017). Characteristics of effective classroom rules: A review of the literature. *Teacher Education & Special Education, 40*(2), 114–127.

Altermatt, E., Jovanovic, J., & Perry, M. (1998). Bias or responsivity? Sex and achievement-level effects on teachers' classroom questioning practices. *Journal of Educational Psychology, 90*(3), 516–527.

Asay, L., & Orgill, M. (2010). Analysis of essential features of inquiry found in articles published in *The Science Teacher*, 1998–2007. *Journal of Science Teacher Education, 21*(1), 57–79.

Berry, A. (2020). Disrupting to driving: Exploring upper primary teachers' perspectives on student engagement. *Teachers and Teaching.* Advance online publication. doi: 10.1080/13540602.2020.1757421

Birch, S. H., & Ladd, G. W. (1997). The teacher–child relationship and children's early school adjustment. *Journal of School Psychology, 35*(1), 61–79.

Brink, C. R. (1935). *Caddie Woodlawn.* New York, NY: Macmillan.

Brookhart, S. (2008). *How to give effective feedback to your students.* Alexandria, VA: ASCD.

Brualdi, A. (1998). *Implementing performance assessment in the classroom.* ERIC/AE Digest [ED423312]. Retrieved from https://files.eric.ed.gov/fulltext/ED423312.pdf

Cameron, C. E., Connor, C. M., & Morrison, F. J. (2005). Effects of teacher organization on classroom functioning. *Journal of School Psychology, 43*(1), 61–85.

Canva. (n.d.). Retrieved from https://www.canva.com/

CAST. (2018). *Universal Design for Learning Guidelines version 2.2.* Retrieved from http://udlguidelines.cast.org

Castek, J., Henry, L., Coiro, J., Leu, D., & Hartman, D. (2015). Research on instruction and assessment in the new literacies of online research and comprehension. In S. Parris & K. Headley, *Comprehension instruction: Research-based best practices* (3rd ed., pp. 324–344). New York, NY: Guilford Press.

Center for Distributed Learning. (2012). *What is accessibility?* Teaching Online Website. Retrieved from https://cdl.ucf.edu/teach/accessibility/

Chen, B., Vargas, J., Thompson, K., & Carter, P. (2014). Screencasts. In B. Chen, A. deNoyelles, & K. Thompson (Eds.), *Teaching online pedagogical repository*. University of Central Florida Center for Distributed Learning. Retrieved from https://topr.online.ucf.edu/screencasts/

Clinton, J., & Dawson, G. (2018). Enfranchising the profession through evaluation: A story from Australia. *Teachers and Teaching, 24*(3), 312–327.

Conrad, P. (1994). *Prairie visions: The life and times of Solomon Butcher*. New York, NY: HarperCollins.

Conroy, M. A., Sutherland, K. S., Snyder, A. L., & Marsh, S. (2008). Classwide interventions: Effective instruction makes a difference. *TEACHING Exceptional Children, 40*(6), 24–30.

Consalvo, A., & Maloch, B. (2015). Keeping the teacher at arm's length: Student resistance in writing conferences in two high school classrooms. *Journal of Classroom Interaction, 50*(2), 120–132.

Cornelius-White, J. (2007). Learner-centered teacher–student relationships are effective: A meta-analysis. *Review of Educational Research, 77,* 113–143.

Cotton, K. (2001). *Classroom questioning.* North West Regional Educational Laboratory. Retrieved from https://educationnorthwest.org/sites/default/files/resources/classroom-questioning-508.pdf

Covey, S. (2008). *The speed of trust: The one thing that changes everything.* New York, NY: Simon & Schuster.

Davies, M., Kiemer, K., & Meissel, K. (2017). Quality talk and dialogic teaching: An examination of a professional development programme on secondary teachers' facilitation of student talk. *British Educational Research Journal, 43*(5), 968–987.

Elliott, K. W., Elliott, J. K., & Spears, S. G. (2018). Teaching on empty. *Principal, 98*(2), 28–29.

Elwell, L., & Lopez Elwell, C. (2020). That's not his name no more. *Leadership, 49*(3), 12–15.

Emmer, E. T., Evertson, C. M., & Anderson, L. M. (1980). Effective classroom management at the beginning of the school year. *The Elementary School Journal, 80*(5), 219–231.

Erdogan, I., & Campbell, T. (2008). Teacher questioning and interaction patterns in classrooms facilitated with differing levels of constructivist teaching practices. *International Journal of Science Education, 30*(14), 1891–1914.

Ericsson, A., & Pool, R. (2016). *Peak: Secrets from the new science of expertise.* Boston, MA: Houghton Mifflin Harcourt.

Evertson, C. M., & Emmer, E. T. (1982). Preventive classroom management. In D. Duke (Ed.), *Helping teachers manage classrooms* (pp. 2–31). Alexandria, VA: ASCD.

Fendick, F. (1990). *The correlation between teacher clarity of communication and student achievement gain: A meta-analysis* (Doctoral dissertation). Retrieved from University of Florida Digital Collections, https://ufdc.ufl.edu/AA00032787/00001

Figley, C. R. (2002). Compassion fatigue: Psychotherapists' chronic lack of self-care. *Journal of Clinical Psychology, 58*(11), 1433–1441.

Fisher, D., Frey, N., Amador, O., & Assof, J. (2019). *The teacher clarity playbook: A hands-on guide to creating learning intentions and success criteria for organized, effective instruction.* Thousand Oaks, CA: Corwin.

Fisher, D., Frey, N., & Hattie, J. (2016). *Visible learning in literacy.* Thousand Oaks, CA: Corwin.

Fisher, D., Frey, N., & Lapp, D. (2009). *In a reading state of mind: Brain research, teacher modeling, and comprehension instruction.* Newark, DE: International Reading Association.

Fisher, D., Frey, N., & Pumpian, I. (2011). No penalties for practice. *Educational Leadership, 69*(3), 46–51.

Fisher, D., Frey, N., Quaglia, R. J., Smith, D., & Lande, L. L. (2018). *Engagement by design: Creating learning environments where students thrive.* Thousand Oaks, CA: Corwin.

Fisher, D., Frey, N., & Smith, D. (2020). *Teacher credibility and collective efficacy playbook.* Thousand Oaks, CA: Corwin.

Fitzpatrick, J. (2016). Pop-up pedagogy: Sharing resources and generating teachable moments with students. *Journal of Family & Consumer Sciences, 108*(1), 52–54.

Fredricks, J. A., Blumenfeld, P. C., & Paris, A. H. (2004). School engagement: Potential of the concept, state of the evidence. *Review of Educational Research, 74*(1), 59–109.

Frey, N., Fisher, D., & Gonzalez, A. (2013). *Teaching with tablets.* Alexandria, VA: ASCD Arias.

Frey, N., Fisher, D., & Hattie, J. (2018). *Developing assessment-capable visible learners: Maximizing skill, will, and thrill.* Thousand Oaks, CA: Corwin.

Good, T. (1987). Two decades of research on teacher expectations. *Journal of Teacher Education, 38*(4), 32–47.

Gordon, R. (2004). The social system as a site of disaster impact and resource for recovery. *Australian Journal of Emergency Management, 19*(4), 16–22.

Gregory, K. (1997). *Across the wide and lonesome prairie: The diary of Hattie Campbell.* New York, NY: Scholastic.

Hall, R. M., & Sandler, B. R. (1982). *The classroom climate: A chilly one for women?* Retrieved from https://files.eric.ed.gov/fulltext/ED215628.pdf

Hattie, J. (2018). *250 Influences chart.* Retrieved from https://www.visiblelearning.com/content/visible-learning-research

Hattie, J., & Timperley, H. (2007). The power of feedback. *Review of Educational Research, 77*(1), 81–112.

Hattie, J., & Zierer, K. (2018). *10 mindframes for Visible Learning: Teaching for success.* New York, NY: Routledge.

Hendrickx, M. M. H. G., Mainhard, T., Oudman, S., Boor-Klip, H. J., & Brekelmans, M. (2017). Teacher behavior and peer liking and disliking: The teacher as a social referent for peer status. *Journal of Educational Psychology, 109*(4), 546–558.

Hoy, W. K., & Tschannen-Moran, M. (2003). The conceptualization and measurement of faculty trust in schools. In W. Hoy & C. Miskel (Eds.), *Studies in leading and organizing schools* (pp. 181–208). Greenwich, CT: Information Age Publishing.

Johnson, S. D., Suriya, C., Yoon, S. W., Berrett, J. V., & La Fleur, J. (2002). Team development and group processes of virtual learning teams. *Computer & Education, 39*(4), 379–393.

Levin, T., & Long, R. (1981). *Effective instruction.* Alexandria, VA: ASCD.

Loom. (n.d.). Retrieved from https://www.loom.com/

Ma, W., Adesope, O. O., Nesbit, J. C., & Liu, Q. (2014). Intelligent tutoring systems and learning outcomes: A meta-analysis. *Journal of Educational Psychology, 106,* 901–918.

Matsumura, L. C., Slater, S. C., & Crosson, A. (2008). Classroom climate, rigorous instruction and curriculum, and students' interactions in urban middle schools. *Elementary School Journal, 108*(4), 293–312.

Mehrabian, A. (1971). *Silent messages.* Belmont, CA: Wadsworth.

Mohr, K. A. J. (1998). Teacher talk: A summary analysis of effective teachers' discourse during primary literacy lessons. *Journal of Classroom Interaction, 33*(2), 16–23.

National Center for Educational Statistics. (2019). *Fast facts: Distance learning.* Retrieved from https://nces.ed.gov/fastfacts/display.asp?id=80

Nystrand, M., Gamoran, A., & Carbonaro, W. (1998). *Towards an ecology of learning: The case of classroom discourse and its effects on writing in high school English and social studies* (No. 11001). Albany, NY: National Research Center on English Learning & Achievement.

Nystrand, M., Wu, M., Gamoran, A., Zeiser, S., & Long, D. (2001). *Questions in time: Investigating the structure and dynamics of unfolding classroom discourse* (No. 14005). Albany, NY: The National Research Center on English Learning & Achievement.

O'Dell, S. (1970). *Sing down the moon.* Boston, MA: Houghton Mifflin.

Osofsky, J. D., Osofsky, H. J., & Harris, W. W. (2007). Katrina's children: Social policy considerations for children in disasters. *Society for Research in Child Development, 21*(1), 3–18.

Palincsar, A. S., & Brown, A. L. (1984). Reciprocal teaching of comprehension-fostering and comprehension-monitoring activities. *Cognition and Instruction, 1*(2), 117–175.

Palmer, D., Dixon, J., & Archer, J. (2016). Using situational interest to enhance individual interest and science-related behaviours. *Research in Science Education, 47,* 731–753.

Pane, J. F., McCaffrey, D. F., Kalra, N., & Zhou, A. J. (2008). Effects of student displacement in Louisiana during the first academic year after the hurricanes of 2005. *Journal of Education for Students Placed at Risk, 13*(2/3), 168–211.

PechaKucha 20x20. (n.d.). Retrieved from https://www.pechakucha.com/

Pfifferling, J., & Gilley, K. (2000). Overcoming compassion fatigue. *Family Practice Management, 7*(4), 39–44.

Pixabay. (n.d.). Retrieved from https://pixabay.com/

Porche, D. J. (2009). *Emergent leadership during a natural disaster: A narrative analysis of an acute health care organization's leadership* (Doctoral dissertation). Capella University. Retrieved from https://pqdtopen.proquest.com/doc/305162131.html?FMT=AI&pubnum=3378903

Priniski, S. J., Hecht, C. A., & Harackiewicz, J. M. (2018). Making learning personally meaningful: A new framework for relevance research. *Journal of Experimental Education, 86*, 11–29.

Randolph, J. J. (2007). Meta-analysis of the research on response cards: Effects on test achievement, quiz achievement, participation, and off-task behavior. *Journal of Positive Behavior Interventions, 9*(2), 113–128.

Rosenshine, B. (2008). *Five meanings of direct instruction*. Lincoln, IL: Center on Innovation & Improvement.

Ryan, P. M. (1998). *Riding freedom*. New York, NY: Scholastic.

Sacerdote, B. (2012). When the saints go marching out: Long-term outcomes for student evacuees of Hurricanes Katrina and Rita. *American Economic Journal: Applied Economics, 4*(1), 109–135.

Sayyah, M., Shirbandi, K., Saki Malehi, A., & Rahim, F. (2017). Use of a problem-based learning teaching model for undergraduate medical and nursing education: A systematic review and meta-analysis. *Advances in Medical Education and Practice, 8*, 691–700. doi:10.2147/amep.s143694

Shomoossi, N. (2004). The effect of teachers' questioning behavior on EFL classroom interaction: A classroom research study. *The Reading Matrix, 4*(2), 96–104.

South Australia Department for Education and Child Development. (2019). *Transforming tasks: Designing tasks where students do the thinking*. Office for Education. Retrieved from https://acleadersresource.sa.edu.au/features/transforming-tasks/Transforming_tasks_overview_chart.pdf

Staarman, J. K. (2009). The joint negotiation of ground rules: Establishing a shared collaborative practice with new educational technology. *Language and Education, 23*(1), 79–95.

Stamm, B. H. (2010). *The concise ProQOL manual* (2nd ed.). Pocatello, ID: ProQOL.org.

Stanovich, K. E. (1986). Matthew effects in reading: Some consequences of individual differences in the acquisition of literacy. *Reading Research Quarterly, 22*, 360–407.

U.S. Department of Education, National Center for Education Statistics. (2019, December). *Digest of education statistics 2019*, Table 311.15. Retrieved from https://nces.ed.gov/programs/digest/d19/tables/dt19_311.15.asp

Van der Kolk, B. (2015). *The body keeps the score: Brain, mind, and body in the healing of trauma*. New York, NY: Penguin.

von Frank, V. (2010). Trust matters: For educators, parents, and students. *Tools for Schools, 14*(1), 1–3.

Voerman, L. A., Meijer, P., Korthagen, F., & Simons, R. P. (2012). Types and frequencies of feedback interventions in classroom interaction in secondary education. *Teaching & Teacher Education, 28*(8), 1107–1115.

Wangberg, J. K. (1996). Teaching with a passion. *American Entomologist, 42*(4), 199–200.

Wiliam, D. (2020). *Formative assessment and online teaching*. Australian Institute for Teaching and School Leadership. Retrieved from https://www.aitsl.edu.au/secondary/comms/australianteacherresponse/formative-assessment-and-online-teaching

Windschitl, M. (2019). Disciplinary literacy versus doing school. *Journal of Adolescent & Adult Literacy, 63*(1), 7–13.

Wisniewski, B., Zierer, K., & Hattie, J. (2020). The power of feedback revisited: A meta-analysis of educational feedback research. *Frontiers in Psychology, 10,* 1–14.

Zierer, K., Lachner, C., Tögel, J., & Weckend, D. (2018). Teacher mindframes from an educational science perspective. *Educational Sciences, 8*(4), 209–221.

Zumbrunn, S., Marrs, S., & Mewborn, C. (2016). Toward a better understanding of student perceptions of writing feedback: A mixed methods study. *Reading & Writing, 29*(2), 349–370.

INDEX

ABOUT THE AUTHORS

Douglas Fisher, MPH, PhD, is professor and chair of educational leadership at San Diego State University. Previously he taught American Sign Language and health education courses in San Diego community colleges. In addition, he is a school credentialed administrator in California and the author of several textbooks used in teacher education courses.

Nancy Frey, PhD, is professor of educational leadership at San Diego State University. Previously, she was professor of teacher education and a special education teacher. She is the author of over 150 journal articles and 60 books on quality teaching and learning.

(Continued)

John Almarode, PhD, is an associate professor of education and executive director of teaching and learning. He has worked with schools all over the world. John works alongside his colleagues in the College of Education with the Teacher Education, Teacher Induction, Teacher Leadership, and Educational Partnerships. John has authored multiple articles, reports, book chapters, and over a dozen books on teaching and learning.

John Hattie, PhD, is an award-winning education researcher and best-selling author with nearly 30 years of experience examining what works best in student learning and achievement. His research, better known as Visible Learning®, synthesizes more than 1,600 meta-analyses comprising more than 95,000 studies involving 300+ million students around the world. His notable publications include *Visible Learning, Visible Learning for Teachers, Visible Learning and the Science of How We Learn,* and *10 Mindframes for Visible Learning.*

A SAGE Publishing Company

Helping educators make the greatest impact

CORWIN HAS ONE MISSION: to enhance education through intentional professional learning.

We build long-term relationships with our authors, educators, clients, and associations who partner with us to develop and continuously improve the best evidence-based practices that establish and support lifelong learning.